I0831063

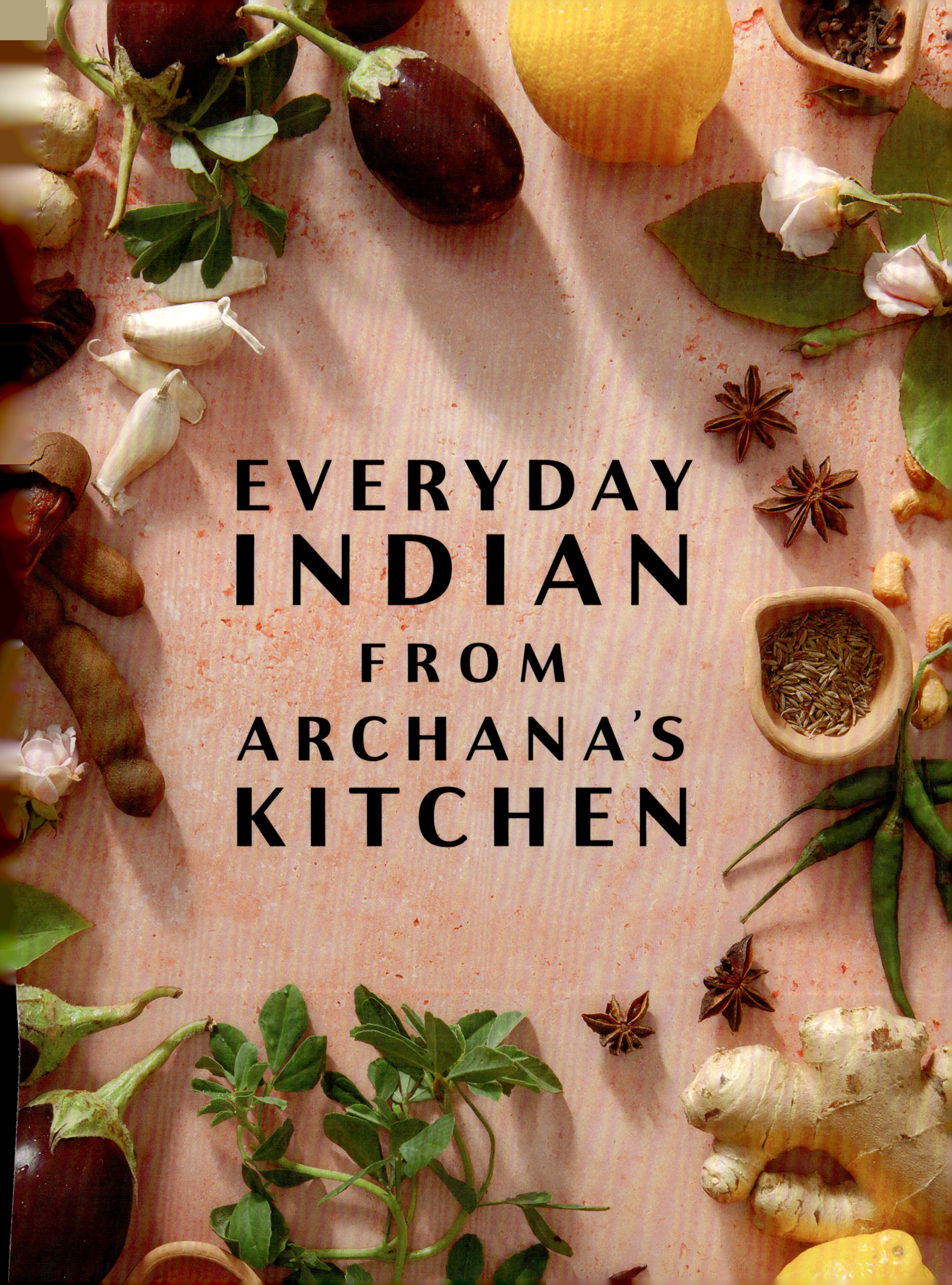

EVERYDAY INDIAN FROM ARCHANA'S KITCHEN

EVERYDAY
INDIAN
FROM ARCHANA'S KITCHEN

100 SIMPLE RECIPES FOR BUSY HOME COOKS

ARCHANA DOSHI

weldonowen

CONTENTS

INTRODUCTION

The Essence of Everyday Indian Food

A CELEBRATION OF FLAVOR AND TRADITION

Indian food is not just about cooking—it's about culture, heritage, and the joy of gathering around a hearty meal. The beauty of everyday Indian food lies in its balance of flavors, diversity of ingredients, and deep-rooted traditions passed down through generations. From a simple dal and sabzi to an elaborate *thali*, every meal is designed to be nourishing, flavorful, and comforting.

So, what makes everyday Indian food so special? Let's dive into its core elements.

A BALANCED PLATE

Indian home cooking is deeply rooted in traditional wisdom passed on from generation to generation, ensuring that each meal is wholesome and nutritionally balanced. A typical everyday Indian meal consists of:

- **Sabzi (vegetable stir-fries and curries):** Seasonal vegetables cooked with aromatic spices and herbs
- **Dal or legume-based dishes:** Lentils, chickpeas, or kidney beans, which provide plant-based protein
- **Roti, paratha, or rice:** A staple carb component is added for sustenance and satisfaction
- **Chutneys, pickles, and raitas:** Flavor boosters that enhance digestion and add variety
- **Salads and accompaniments:** Fresh, raw vegetables, sometimes tempered, to bring contrast to the meal
- **Desserts:** Typically not part of an everyday meal but served during special weekend meals, occasions, and festivals, often made from everyday pantry ingredients and pair sweet flavors with delicate spices

This thoughtful combination ensures that meals are not just filling but also holistically nourishing, keeping the body and mind energized.

A VARIED CULINARY LANDSCAPE

India is home to a rich culinary diversity, where every state, and sometimes even every household, has its unique way of preparing food. Some highlights include:

- **North India:** Creamy dals, rich curries, and tandoori breads, such as naan and paratha
- **South India:** Rice-based dishes, coconut-infused curries, and fermented foods, such as *dosa* and *idli*
- **East India:** Mustard-flavored fish curries, hearty lentils, and sweets such as *rasgulla*

- **West India:** Spiced vegetable dishes, millet rotis, and tangy chutneys

Every region contributes a different spice profile, cooking technique, and key ingredient, yet all meals revolve around the idea of comfort and sustenance.

A WEALTH OF SPICES AND HERBS

No Indian meal is complete without spices—they are the heart and soul of Indian cooking. Everyday dishes are seasoned with a combination of:

- **Asafetida (hing):** A digestive aid, commonly used in dals and sabzis
- **Cumin, coriander, and cilantro:** Earthy and mildly citrusy, used in almost every dish
- **Ginger and garlic:** The flavor base for most curries and stir-fries
- **Mustard seeds and curry leaves:** Essential in tempering
- **Turmeric:** Anti-inflammatory and earthy in flavor

The key to Indian cooking is layering spices—tempering whole spices in oil, roasting ground spices, and using fresh herbs like cilantro and mint for a final touch of freshness.

A RELIANCE ON TRADITIONAL COOKING TECHNIQUES

Indian food may seem complex, but everyday meals rely on simple yet effective cooking techniques that enhance flavor and nutrition:

- ***Dum* cooking:** A slow-cooking method used for biryanis and rich gravies
- **Sautéing and roasting (*bhuna*):** Slow-cooking onions, tomatoes, and spices to build depth of flavor
- **Steaming and fermentation:** *Idlis*, *dosas*, and *dhoklas* benefit from natural fermentation, which enhances taste and is good for gut health
- **Tempering and seasoning (*tadka*):** Heating spices in ghee or oil to release their aromas; commonly used in dals and curries

These methods are time-tested and efficient, making even the simplest ingredients taste extraordinary.

A LOVE OF FRESH AND SEASONAL INGREDIENTS

Indian cooking revolves around fresh, seasonal, and local ingredients, ensuring that every meal is nutritious and aligned with nature's cycle. Some key principles include:

- **Avoiding processed ingredients:** Homemade spice blends, freshly ground flours, and natural dairy products are preferred over store-bought alternatives
- **Eating seasonal fruits and vegetables:** Summer brings cooling cucumbers and mangoes, whereas winter offers root vegetables and leafy greens
- **Using whole grains and millets:** Whole wheat, rice, jowar (sorghum), and bajra form the foundation of Indian staples

The emphasis on freshness and minimal wastage ensures that meals are not only delicious but also sustainable.

A JOY IN EVERYDAY HOME COOKING

Despite the variety and depth of Indian cuisine, home-cooked meals remain simple, satisfying, and made with love. A typical day's meal could be as comforting as dal *chawal* with a dollop of ghee, or as elaborate as a *thali* with multiple curries, breads, and condiments.

Cooking at home brings a sense of connection—to our families, our traditions, and our roots. Whether it's the comforting aroma of a slow-simmered dal or the crisp sound of parathas sizzling on the *tawa*, every dish tells a story.

A FINAL THOUGHT

Bringing Indian Food to Your Table

Everyday Indian food is vibrant, versatile, and deeply nourishing. It's not just about what's on the plate but also about the warmth and tradition that go into every meal. Whether you're new to Indian cooking or looking to expand your home menu, remember:

- Keep it simple and seasonal
- Balance spices, textures, and flavors
- Enjoy the process of cooking and sharing meals

With this book, I invite you to explore the joy of everyday Indian food, bringing the essence of home-cooked Indian meals into your kitchen!

A COMPREHENSIVE GUIDE
to the Everyday Indian Pantry

Few things in life evoke the warmth of home as vividly as walking into a kitchen redolent with the scent of spices, sizzling temperings, and the comforting aroma of simmering dals. In an Indian household, the pantry doesn't just hold ingredients—it safeguards family traditions, memories, and a collective culinary identity. Each spice jar, each can of lentils, and each package of rice is part of a tapestry that has been woven over centuries, bridging generations through the act of cooking and sharing meals.

Growing up, I remember how my mother's pantry was the heart of her home. Jars labeled in her neat handwriting lined the shelves, bursting with vibrant colors—from the golden hue of turmeric to the deep red of chili powder. These jars, and the rituals of measuring, roasting, and grinding that surrounded them, felt like a secret gateway to the essence of Indian food. When she opened a new box of cumin seeds or dal, she would breathe in the aroma, as if reacquainting herself with an old friend. It was in these small details that I realized how integral a well-stocked pantry is to creating everyday Indian dishes—with each ingredient carrying its own story, flavor profile, and nutritional properties.

Your Indian pantry is your culinary playground—a place where spices, grains, herbs, and oils come together in infinite combinations to create the soul-satisfying dishes India is famed for. Every jar, package, or can is a piece of history and a dash of innovation, reminding us that Indian cooking is always evolving yet steadfastly tied to its roots. By stocking these essential ingredients and understanding how they interact, you'll have the tools to explore the wonders of everyday Indian cuisine—from a quick dal and sabzi to a lavish feast fit for royal guests.

Embrace the colors, aromas, and personalities of each pantry staple—and soon enough, you'll find joy in the simple act of opening a spice jar, breathing in its fragrance, and imagining the possibilities of the meal ahead.

Following, we'll explore eight key categories of pantry essentials—spices, lentils, grains, oils, herbs, sweeteners, nuts, and condiments. Understanding each ingredient's role, flavor, and cultural context is the first step toward effortlessly bringing the magic of everyday Indian cooking into your kitchen.

SPICES AND SEASONINGS
The Soul of Indian Cooking

Indian food's distinctive character comes largely from the intricate interplay of spices. From the humble pinch of asafetida that transforms a lentil soup, to the fiery red chili powder that gives an otherwise mild curry a bold punch, spices breathe life into every dish. For many of us, just the smell of sputtering cumin seeds in hot ghee can evoke childhood memories of bustling family kitchens and comforting home-cooked meals.

Why They Matter

Each spice has a unique flavor profile, from earthy cumin to pungent mustard seeds. They can be tempered (*tadka*), ground, or added whole, affecting the dish's final taste and aroma. Many spices also have therapeutic properties, underscoring the ancient link between Ayurveda and Indian food.

Asafetida (*hing*)

- **Flavor:** Strong sulfurous aroma when raw; becomes pleasantly savory and onion-like when fried in oil
- **Usage:** A pinch in lentil-based dishes, *sambar*, and vegetarian curries can transform the flavor profile
- **Tip:** Store in an airtight container, as its aroma can be quite pervasive

Bay leaves (*tej patta*)

- **Flavor profile:** Sweet, herbal, and slightly floral
- **Usage:** Common in biryanis, *pulaos*, and slow-cooked gravies, providing subtle aromatic notes

Cardamom (*elaichi*)

- **Varieties:**
  - Green cardamom: Sweet, floral; used in desserts, teas, and some gravies
  - Black cardamom: Smoky, bold; used in rich curries, biryanis, and garam masala
- **Usage:** Whole pods often cracked and added to hot oil or ghee, or seeds ground into spice blends

Cinnamon (*dalchini*)

- **Flavor:** Sweet-woody aroma with a light spice
- **Usage:** Added to hot oil or ghee in the initial tempering phase of *pulaos*, curries, or masala chai

Cloves (*laung*)

- **Flavor:** Intensely warm, sweet, and slightly bitter
- **Usage:** A key component in garam masala, biryanis, and flavored rice dishes. A little goes a long way thanks to its strong flavor

Coriander powder (*dhania* powder)

- **Flavor:** Mildly citrusy, warm, and slightly sweet
- **Usage:** Foundational spice in most North Indian curries and dry sabzis; pairs well with cumin
- **Tip:** Toast whole coriander seeds and grind them at home for a fresher taste

Cumin powder (*jeera* powder)

- **Flavor:** Warm, earthy, and nutty
- **Usage:** Enhances dals, raitas, curries, and spice blends like garam masala
- **Tip:** Lightly roast cumin seeds before grinding for an even richer flavor

Curry leaves (*kadi patta*)

- **Flavor:** Refreshing, citrusy, and slightly nutty aroma
- **Usage:** Essential in South Indian tempering; added to hot oil along with mustard seeds, imparting a unique flavor to dishes like *sambar* and chutneys

Dried fenugreek leaves (*kasuri methi*)

- **Flavor:** Dried fenugreek leaves, with a bitter-sweet aroma
- **Usage:** Typically sprinkled at the end to give dishes like paneer butter masala a distinctive earthy note

Dried red chiles

- **Flavor:** Kashmiri (mild, with a vibrant color), Byadgi (mild to medium), Guntur (hot)
- **Usage:** Used whole in tempering or ground into pastes and chutneys for both heat and color

Fenugreek seeds (*methi dana*)

- **Flavor:** Distinctly bitter, with a sweet afternote when lightly roasted
- **Usage:** Adds complexity to pickles, spice powders, and curries, such as *methi kadhi*
- **Health benefits:** Known to aid digestion and to help regulate blood sugar levels

Garam masala

- **Flavor:** Aromatic blend of multiple spices (cinnamon, cardamom, cloves, black pepper, among others)
- **Usage:** Typically added toward the end of cooking to preserve its aroma; a key finishing touch for many North Indian dishes
- **Tip:** Homemade garam masala brings a fresher aroma compared with store-bought varieties

Mustard seeds (*rai* or *sarso*)

- **Flavor:** Sharp, pungent when cracked in oil; mildly nutty after cooking
- **Usage:** Integral to South Indian tempering (*tadka*) in *sambar*, *rasam*, chutneys, and pickles
- **Tip:** Wait for them to pop in hot oil to unleash their nutty flavor

Red chili powder (*lal mirch*)

- **Flavor:** Ranges from mildly hot (Kashmiri chile) to very spicy (Byadgi or Guntur chile)
- **Usage:** Sprinkled into curries, spice mixes, and marinades to add heat and color
- **Tip:** Adjust the quantity based on your spice tolerance; Kashmiri chile is favored for its vibrant color without excessive heat

Turmeric (*haldi*)

- **Flavor:** Earthy, mildly bitter, and peppery
- **Usage:** Often added early in cooking to release color and merge flavors; a go-to spice in curries, dals, and sabzis
- **Health benefits:** Known for anti-inflammatory properties due to its active compound, curcumin

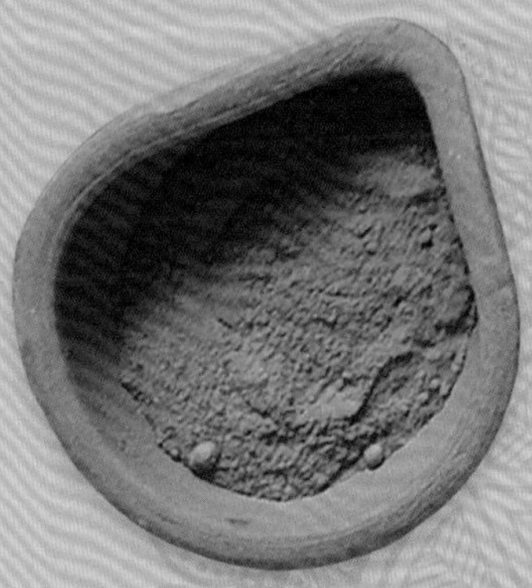

LENTILS AND LEGUMES

The Protein Backbone

Whereas spices provide taste and aroma, lentils and legumes supply the nutritional heft in Indian cuisine. Whether it's a comforting bowl of dal *tadka* or a hearty curry like *chole* (chickpeas), these staples ensure that vegetarian meals remain balanced and satisfying. My mother's go-to "comfort food" was always a simple dal-rice combo with a spoonful of homemade ghee—a dish that remains the pinnacle of nourishment and nostalgia for me.

Why They Matter

High in protein, lentils and legumes are especially important in vegetarian diets. They provide a creamy base for dals, thicken sauces, and contribute to a dish's overall texture. Each variety—whether it's *toor*, *moong*, *masoor*, or urad—brings its own distinct taste, color, and cooking time.

Bengal gram split (chana dal)

- **Flavor:** Nutty and firm
- **Usage:** Used in tempering, *kadhi*, and snacks like *dhokla* and *farsan*; also a main ingredient in certain sweets like *chana dal halwa*

Black chana (*kala* chana)

- **Flavor:** Earthier and more fibrous than *kabuli* chana
- **Usage:** Used in curries, sprouts for salads, or stir-fries like black chana *sundal*

Black gram (urad dal)

- **Varieties:** Split (skinned) or whole (with black husk)
- **Usage:** Critical in *idli* and *dosa* batter, *papad*-making, and *dal makhani*. Split urad is used in tempering for many South Indian dishes

Black-eyed peas (*lobia*)

- **Flavor:** Mild, slightly smoky aroma
- **Usage:** Cooked into *lobia* masala or combined with vegetables for a protein-packed salad

Chickpeas (*kabuli* chana)

- Flavor: Mild, nutty
- Usage: Star of *chole bhature* and salads; can also be ground into hummus (fusion adaptation)

Dried and fresh green peas (*matar*)

- **Varieties:** Fresh (seasonal), frozen, or dried
- **Usage:** Popular in *matar* paneer, *pulaos*, and snacks like *ghugni* or *matar kachori*

Kidney beans (*rajma*)

- **Flavor:** Robust, hearty bean commonly used in North Indian *rajma masala*
- **Usage:** Pairs well with steamed rice (*rajma chawal*) for a comforting meal

Pigeon peas (*toor* dal)

- **Flavor:** Mild and slightly sweet; forms the base for *sambar* across South India and dal fry in the North
- **Usage:** Boils quickly; typically tempered with ghee, cumin, mustard seeds, and curry leaves

Red lentils (*masoor* dal)

- **Flavor:** Earthy, cooks to a soft texture
- **Usage:** Ideal for basic dals, soups, and quick one-pot meals; commonly found in Eastern Indian and Nepali cuisine too

Whole and split green gram (*moong* dal)

- **Flavor:** Light and sweet; quick-cooking and easily digestible
- **Usage:** Widely used in *khichdi*, simple dal, and even in sweets like *moong dal halwa*

GRAINS, FLOURS, AND MILLETS

The Everyday Fuel

Few sights are as satisfying as perfectly puffed *phulkas*, or the aroma of steaming basmati rice. Indian meals revolve around these staples—rotis, parathas, puris, and a variety of rice preparations that form the bedrock on which our dals, curries, and chutneys are built. Growing interest in healthy eating has also revived millets like ragi, jowar, and bajra, revered for their nutrient density and ancient heritage.

Why They Matter
These primary carbohydrates are energy food and serve as a neutral backdrop for spicy or rich dishes. Whole wheat flour (*atta*) and different millets enrich the meal with fiber, vitamins, and minerals, whereas rice plays a supporting role in many dishes, from aromatic basmati for biryanis to *sona masuri* for everyday meals.

All-purpose flour (*maida*)

- **Usage:** For naan, bhatura, and some sweets; yields softer textures but is less nutritious than *atta*

Broken wheat (*daliya*)

- **Flavor:** Mild and nutty
- **Usage:** Nutritious breakfast porridge, healthy *khichdi*, or *upma*; good for diabetic-friendly diets

Flattened rice (*poha*)

- **Usage:** Popular in breakfast dishes, such as *kanda poha*; also used in snacks like *chivda*; absorbs water quickly, so perfect when making meals in a hurry

Millets (jowar, bajra, ragi, foxtail, and others)

- **Usage:** Rotis, porridges, healthy alternatives to rice or wheat
- **Health benefits:** High in fiber and minerals; gluten free

Rice (*chawal*)

- **Varieties:**
  - **Basmati:** Long-grain, fragrant; for biryanis, *pulaos*, and special occasions
  - **Sona masuri/Kolam/jeera samba/gobind bhog:** medium-grain and used in everyday cooking
- **Usage:** Staple across many regions; used in *khichdi*, *pongal*, *idli/dosa* batters (when mixed with lentils)

Semolina (*sooji/rava*)

- **Usage:** Used in *upma*, *halwa*, *dhokla*, and crispy *dosa* batters; available in coarse and fine varieties

Whole wheat flour (*atta*)

- **Usage:** Foundation for rotis, parathas, and puris
- **Health benefits:** Higher in fiber and nutrients than most refined flours

FATS AND OILS

The Medium of Flavor

The moment mustard seeds pop in hot oil or ghee, releasing their nutty fragrance, you know something delicious is underway. In Indian cooking, the choice of fat—be it ghee, mustard oil, coconut oil, or peanut oil—can dramatically change a dish's flavor profile and regional identity. My grandmother always insisted on desi ghee for final drizzles, claiming it "brings out the soul of the dal," and I couldn't agree more.

Why They Matter
Ghee lends a rich, luxurious note to sweets, dals, and rotis. Mustard oil is emblematic of North and East Indian cuisines, whereas coconut oil reigns supreme in South India. Each oil or fat has a specific smoke point, impacting how dishes are tempered or fried.

Coconut oil

- **Flavor:** Mildly sweet coconut scent
- **Usage:** Staple in Kerala and coastal areas; used in fish curries and vegetarian dishes for an authentic taste

Ghee (clarified butter)

- **Flavor:** Rich, nutty aroma; considered sacred in Indian culture
- **Usage:** Used for tempering, sweets, and to finish dishes with a spoonful for extra richness

Mustard oil

- **Flavor:** Pungent, sharp aroma
- **Usage:** Integral to Bengali, Punjabi, and Rajasthani cuisines; used in pickling too

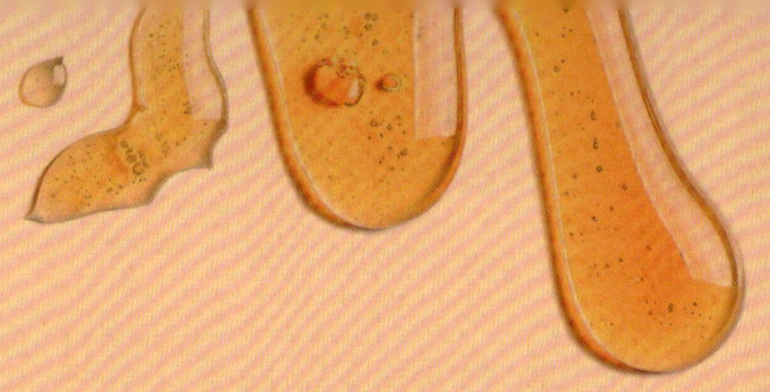

Peanut oil

- **Usage:** Common in Gujarat and Maharashtra for frying and general cooking; has a higher smoke point

Refined vegetable oils (sunflower, canola, rice bran, and others)

- **Usage:** Neutral flavor; widely used for everyday cooking

HERBS AND LEAVES

Fresh Fragrance in Every Bite

A handful of chopped cilantro or a couple of mint sprigs may appear modest, but these fresh herbs lift an entire dish from good to memorable. The aromatic burst of curry leaves sizzling in oil is an unmistakable hallmark of South Indian cooking, whereas fresh *methi* (fenugreek leaves) transforms simple breads into flavorful *theplas*. These seemingly small additions encapsulate nature's brightness in everyday meals.

Why They Matter

Coriander, cilantro, and mint are the backbone of refreshing chutneys. Fenugreek leaves (fresh or dried) add a subtle bitter note that balances richer flavors, whereas herbs often finish a dish, infusing a final layer of aroma and vibrancy.

Cilantro (*dhania patta*)

- **Usage:** Garnish or ground into chutneys; bright and citrusy notes
- **Tip:** Store stems separately, as they're great for stocks and dals

Fenugreek leaves (fresh *methi*)

- **Flavor:** Slightly bitter, but transforms to a subtle sweetness when cooked
- **Usage:** Sautéed into sabzis, kneaded into parathas; pairs well with potatoes and paneer

Mint leaves (*pudina*)

- **Usage:** Refreshing flavor for mint chutney, biryani, raitas, and drinks
- **Tip:** Best used fresh to preserve the aroma

NATURAL SWEETENERS AND FLAVORS

Balancing the Palate

Indian cuisine masterfully balances sweet, sour, salty, and spicy elements, and sweeteners are essential to this alchemy. Jaggery (gur) is more than just sugar—its caramellike depth complements curries and sweets alike, whereas honey finds its place in health drinks and lighter dishes. Meanwhile, saffron strands, rose water, and *kewra* essence bring delicate floral notes to festive treats and special rice preparations.

Why They Matter

Jaggery offers mineral content and a nuanced sweetness in comparison to refined sugar. Rose (*kewra* water) evokes Mughlai extravagance in desserts and biryanis. Saffron adds a golden color and subtle perfume, elevating dishes to a special-occasion status.

Honey

- **Usage:** In health drinks, some marinades, or fusion desserts; known for its natural sweetness and distinct flavor

Jaggery (gur)

- **Flavor:** Rich, molasses-like sweetness
- **Usage:** Key in sweet-sour curries, sweets like *gur papdi*, and certain dals for balance

Rose water (*kewra* water)

- **Flavor:** Floral
- **Usage:** Essential in certain Mughlai gravies, biryanis, and desserts like *gulab jamun* syrup; used sparingly for aroma

Saffron (*kesar*)

- **Usage:** Infused in milk-based sweets, biryanis, and special dishes for a royal golden hue and subtle flavor
- **Tip:** Soak strands in warm water or milk before adding

Sugar

- **Usage:** For desserts, sweet beverages, and occasional balancing of spicy or tangy flavors

NUTS AND SEEDS

Textural and Nutritional Powerhouses

Whether it's the crunch of cashews in a royal curry or the creaminess of almonds in a rich korma gravy, nuts and seeds are commonly used to thicken sauces, garnish sweets, or add textural contrast. Peanuts are pivotal in chutneys, whereas sesame seeds (til) feature prominently in sweets, seasoning breads, and certain chutneys. For me, a bowl of any Indian dessert garnished with chopped pistachios instantly feels festive.

Why They Matter
Nuts and seeds provide healthy fats, protein, and a sumptuous texture to a variety of dishes. They are integral to both savory gravies (like korma) and sweet recipes (like *ladoos*) and bring an element of luxury to everyday dishes with minimal effort.

Almonds (*badam*)

- **Flavor:** Mild, slightly nutty
- **Usage:** Soaked, ground into pastes for desserts or gravy bases such as *badami* curry

Cashews (*kaju*)

- **Flavor:** Mildly sweet, creamy texture
- **Usage:** Thickening agent in gravies (*shahi* paneer) and sweets; used as garnish

Peanuts (*moongfali*)

- **Usage:** Peanut chutney, snacks (*farsan*), and ground for thickening curries; also used in tikkas for texture

Pistachios, walnuts, etc.

- **Usage:** Garnishes for sweets, optional in festive or high-end dishes

Raisins (*kishmish*)

- **Usage:** Added to *pulaos*, kormas, and *halwas* for sweet bursts
- **Tip:** Soak in warm water for plumper raisins

Sesame seeds (til)

- **Flavor:** Nutty, intense when toasted
- **Usage:** Til chutney, sweets (til *ladoo*), and sprinkling over breads.

CONDIMENTS AND EXTRAS:

The Burst of Flavors

No Indian meal is truly complete without pickles, chutneys, raitas, or *papads*. These condiments offer contrasting flavors—tangy pickles cut through the richness of curries, mint or peanut chutney adds zing to snacks, and raita cools the palate after a spicy bite. These seemingly "side" elements can transform a meal from ordinary to extraordinary.

Why They Matter
Pickles (achars) are aged in oil and spices, adding tangy heat to balance heavier dishes. Chutneys, fresh or cooked blends of herbs, fruits, or vegetables, are used for brightening and accentuating. Yogurt-based sides, raitas, help temper spiciness and aid digestion.

Chutneys

- **Varieties:** Green chutney, tamarind chutney, coconut chutney—all offer freshness and zing to dishes

Curd/yogurt

- **Usage:** Eaten plain, in raitas, in *kadhi*, or as a marinade base
- **Health benefits:** Packed with probiotics, beneficial for digestion

Indian wafers (*papd/appalam*)

- **Varieties:** Urad dal *papad*, *jeera papad*, masala *papad*
- **Usage:** Lightly roasted or fried for crispy accompaniment to *thalis* or as a starter

Pickles (achar)

- **Varieties:** Mango, lemon, mixed veggies, and more—spicy, tangy elements to perk up meals
- **Tip:** The shelf life varies from a few weeks to years, depending on the oil and spice content, so be mindful

Raitas

- **Varieties:** *Boondi* raita cucumber raita—cooling yogurt-based sides that complement spicy dishes

TOOLS OF THE TRADE

Essential Equipment for Everyday Indian Cooking

When it comes to Indian cooking, great flavor begins not just with the right ingredients, but also with the right equipment. Armed with this essential equipment—from the trusty pressure cooker or electric multi-cooker to the humble *chakla-belan*—you'll be ready to tackle any everyday Indian recipe.

Each tool has its own role in creating the layers of flavor, texture, and aroma that define Indian home cooking. Embrace these tools as your kitchen companions, and you'll find each sizzling *tarka*, each puffed roti, and each perfectly blended chutney becomes a source of joy in your culinary journey.

Explore, experiment, and savor the process—the heartbeat of an Indian kitchen lies in the synergy of these tools and ingredients and the love you bring to your food.

Following is a comprehensive list of must-have tools that will help you prepare everything from quick *dal-chawal* to elaborate feasts.

PRESSURE COOKER

Why It's Important

A cornerstone of Indian kitchens, the pressure cooker significantly reduces cooking time for dals, legumes, and even certain rice dishes. Many families rely on it daily—listening for the whistle to know dinner is on its way.

Tips

- **Size matters:** A 3- to 5-liter cooker suits small to medium families; 6 liters or more is ideal for larger families.
- **Liquid matters:** Always add enough water or stock to prevent scorching.
- **Safety matters:** Let the pressure release naturally for delicate dishes (e.g., dals), or use a quick-release method for sturdier ingredients.

ELECTRIC MULTI-COOKER

Why It's Important

A modern spin on the pressure cooker, the electric multi-cooker offers programmable cooking modes like sauté, slow cook, and yogurt-making. Perfect for "set and forget" cooking, it simplifies multistep Indian recipes into fewer steps.

Tips

- **Adjust times:** Stovetop recipes may need tweaks if using an electric multi-cooker.
- **Layer flavors:** Use the "Sauté" mode first to fry spices or onions before pressure cooking.
- **Create one-pot meals:** These are perfect for making *khichdi*, biryani, and curries without much oversight.

KADAI (INDIAN WOK)

Why It's Important

A thick-bottomed, deep wok is essential for cooking Indian stir-fries, deep-frying snacks, and making curries or dry sabzis. The curved sides allow efficient movement of food and even heat distribution.

Tips

- Choose a heavy-bottomed *kadai* to prevent burning.
- Use to make perfect bhindi masala, *aloo gobi*, or even for frying *pakoras*.

TAWA (FLAT OR CONCAVE GRIDDLE)

Why It's Important

Essential for *phulka*, paratha, *dosas*, and other flatbreads, it ensures even heating, which results in soft and fluffy breads. The griddle can also be used for shallow-frying certain snacks.

Tips

- A cast-iron *tawa* retains heat well and adds seasoning over time.
- The nonstick *tawa* is ideal for cooking *dosa* and *cheelas* and keeps them from sticking to the pan.
- Always keep a separate *tawa* for making rotis and parathas and another *tawa* for making *dosas*.
- Use medium-high heat for rotis or parathas; adjust to high or low, depending on bread thickness.

PANS AND POTS

Saucepans, Stir-Fry Pans, *Tadka* Pan, and Mixing Bowls

Why They're Important

- **Large and Small Saucepans:** Saucepans are necessary for simmering dals or making small curries. Heavy-bottomed pans prevent scorching.
- **Stir-Fry Pans:** If you don't have a *kadai*, these deep pans are great for sautéing vegetables, noodles, and quick curries.
- **Small Pan (*Tadka*):** A small pan is useful for tempering and seasoning. It's ideal for frying spices in oil or ghee (*tadka*). These pans are essential when adding the final flavor burst in dals and certain curries.
- **Mixing Bowls:** Bowls are needed for prepping dough, marinating meats, and mixing batter.

Tips

- Keep a dedicated *tadka* pan to avoid flavor crossover.
- Have at least one medium saucepan and one large saucepan for different batch sizes.
- Stir-fry pans should have high sides to prevent spills.
- Stainless-steel or glass bowls are preferred, as they are easy to clean and don't react with acidic ingredients.

SPICE GRINDER, MORTAR AND PESTLE, OR ELECTRIC MIXER GRINDER

A. Spice Grinder / Mortar and Pestle

Why It's Important

Freshly ground spices elevate Indian dishes; a mortar and pestle offers a traditional, hands-on approach. Electric spice grinders expedite the process for busy cooks.

Tips

- Toast the whole spices briefly before grinding.
- Clean the utensils thoroughly between different spice blends to avoid flavor contamination.

B. Electric Mixer Grinder / Nutri Blender

Why It's Important

An Indian kitchen essential, commonly known as a "mixie," it is used to grind pastes, purées, chutneys, and masalas. Most mixer grinders come with multiple jars, including a large jar for wet grinding (curries, masalas, *idli-dosa* batter) and a smaller jar for dry grinding or making small portions of chutney

Nutri blenders work similarly to grinders, especially for smooth chutneys or blending cooked ingredients into soups or gravies.

Tips

- **Pulse versus grind:** Use short pulses to create coarse textures and continuous grinding for smooth pastes.
- **Cooldown:** Avoid overloading or running the motor for too long; let the grinder cool between large batches.
- **Liquid:** For thick chutneys, add a splash of water or oil to ease grinding.

ROLLING BOARD (*CHAKLA*) AND ROLLING PIN (*BELAN*)

Why They're Important

These tools are integral for rolling out dough into rotis, puris, parathas, and other breads. They ensure even thickness for uniform cooking.

Tips

- Lightly flour both surfaces to prevent sticking.
- Roll gently from the center outward to ensure a consistent shape.

BASIC UTENSILS

Tongs (*Chimta*), Ladles, Slotted Spoons, and Whisks

Why They're Important

- **Tongs (*chimta*):** Handy for flipping rotis over an open flame or lifting hot snacks from oil.
- **Ladle and slotted spoon:** Essential for stirring curries, frying *pakoras*, and draining excess oil.
- **Whisk:** Used to beat yogurt for raitas or for mixing batters.

Tips

- Keep separate spoons and ladles for vegetarian and non-vegetarian dishes, if desired.
- A small whisk is handy for making quick batters, a larger one for thick gravies or *halwas*.

CHAPTER 1

BREAKFAST DELIGHTS

Spicy Mumbai-Style Anda Bhurji with Buttery Pav

SPICY SCRAMBLED EGGS WITH BUTTERED BUNS

YIELD: 4 SERVINGS

Anda Bhurji, a popular Mumbai street food, is a delicious and spicy scrambled-egg dish cooked with onions, tomatoes, green chiles, and fragrant spices. This quick and flavorful dish is a staple in Maharashtrian cuisine, often enjoyed as a hearty breakfast or a comforting meal any time of the day.

Unlike regular scrambled eggs, Mumbai-style Anda Bhurji is packed with bold flavors, making it a favorite among egg lovers.

4 eggs (*anda*)

Kosher salt

2 teaspoons pav bhaji masala

¼ teaspoon turmeric powder

3 tablespoons butter, softened

1-inch piece fresh ginger, peeled and finely grated

1 onion, finely chopped

1 green bell pepper, cored and finely chopped

2 green chiles, finely chopped

1 tomato, finely chopped

6 sprigs cilantro, finely chopped

4 pav buns (or burger buns)

In a large mixing bowl, whisk together the eggs until light and fluffy. Add the salt, to taste, the *pav bhaji* masala, and turmeric powder. Whisk until well combined.

Preheat a stir-fry pan over medium heat. Melt 1 tablespoon of butter, then add the grated ginger, chopped onion, bell pepper, and green chiles. Sauté until the onion and pepper are soft and tender, 2 to 3 minutes. Stir in the tomato and sauté until the tomato softens, 2 to 3 minutes.

Finally, add in the egg mixture to make the Anda Bhurji. Keep stirring the mixture continuously until you begin to see the eggs coming together and are cooked through. Stir in 1 tablespoon of butter and the cilantro and turn off the heat.

To make the *pav* (butter buns): Slice the buns in half and spread the remaining tablespoon of softened butter on one side of each bun. Place them in a preheated skillet and toast over medium heat until golden brown and crisp on both sides.

Sandwich the *anda* in between the buns or serve side by side.

PAIRING SUGGESTIONS

For a complete, satisfying meal, serve with masala chai or lassi.

Kothamalli Rava Upma

CORIANDER-FLAVORED SEMOLINA BREAKFAST

YIELD: 4 SERVINGS

I make Kothamalli Rava Upma whenever I need a quick, feel-good breakfast. It's the regular semolina upma I grew up with, but brightened by a handful of fresh coriander (*kothamalli*). The *rava* is lightly toasted, then cooked with ginger, green chiles, and a fragrant tadka of mustard seeds and curry leaves. A swirl of coriander purée turns everything a cheerful green and fills the kitchen with a garden-fresh aroma.

- 15 sprigs cilantro, coarsely chopped
- 1-inch piece fresh ginger, peeled and finely chopped
- 2 green chiles, finely chopped
- Kosher salt
- 1 teaspoon sugar
- 1 tablespoon sunflower or canola oil
- 1 teaspoon mustard seeds
- 1 teaspoon white urad dal (split)
- 1 sprig curry leaves
- 1 onion, finely chopped
- 1 cup fine semolina (*sooji/rava*)
- 1 lemon, juiced
- 2 tablespoons ghee

Grind the cilantro, ginger, and green chiles into a smooth paste using a mortar and pestle. Add a little water, as needed. Set aside.

Heat 3 cups of water in a saucepan over high heat; add the salt, to taste, and the sugar. Bring to a boil and stir until the sugar dissolves. Turn the heat to low and keep the water simmering.

To make the *upma*, heat the oil in a heavy-bottomed saucepan. Add the mustard seeds and urad dal and let roast until the dal turns golden brown and crisp. Add the curry leaves and onion and cook until the onion is soft and translucent.

Once the onion is softened, add the semolina and roast for 3 to 4 minutes, until you get a lightly roasted aroma. Stir in the cilantro paste.

Gradually add the hot water and keep stirring the *upma* until all the water is absorbed.

Stir in the lemon juice, cover, and cook for 3 minutes. Turn off the heat. Add the ghee and stir. Check the taste and adjust the salt accordingly. Serve hot.

PAIRING SUGGESTIONS

For a delicious breakfast, serve it along with coconut chutney and a hot cup of coffee or fresh orange juice.

Gujarati Bhaat Na Muthiya Dhokla

SAVORY STEAMED RICE DUMPLINGS

YIELD: 4 SERVINGS (5 *MUTHIAS* PER SERVING)

Bhaat Na Muthiya Dhokla is a traditional Gujarati delicacy made using leftover rice, gram flour, and spices, then steamed to perfection. These soft, fluffy, and mildly spiced dumplings are a fantastic way to repurpose rice into a wholesome and delicious snack. Light yet satisfying, they are perfect for breakfast, teatime, or even a light dinner.

This dish hails from the Gujarati region and carries the signature balance of savory, slightly tangy, and mildly sweet flavors that make it truly special.

¼ large calabash (*lauki* or *doodhi*), for ½ cup grated gourd

2 cups short- or long-grain cooked rice

½ cup gram flour (*besan*)

1-inch piece fresh ginger, peeled and finely grated

½ teaspoon turmeric powder

¼ teaspoon asafetida

½ teaspoon red chili powder

6 sprigs cilantro, finely chopped

Kosher salt

1 tablespoon sunflower or canola oil, plus more for greasing

SEASONING

1 teaspoon sunflower or canola oil

1 teaspoon mustard seeds

1 teaspoon sesame seeds

1 sprig curry leaves, coarsely torn

2 tablespoons fresh coconut, grated, for garnish

6 sprigs cilantro, finely chopped, for garnish

RICE TIP

- Save leftover rice to use in this recipe.

Fill a steamer with water and grease the steamer plates.

Peel and grate one-quarter of a large calabash to produce ½ cup of grated gourd. Squeeze out excess water. Cover and store the remaining calabash in the refrigerator.

In a large bowl, combine the grated calabash, rice, gram flour, grated ginger, turmeric powder, asafetida, red chili powder, cilantro, salt, and 1 tablespoon of oil. Mash well using a masher or your hands. The *muthia* mixture will look like a firm ball of dough.

Divide the mixture into 20 equal portions and shape them into ovals, or shape them into longer logs and cut them into rounds after they are steamed.

Place the dumplings 1 inch apart on the greased plates and steam on high heat for 15 minutes. Turn off the heat and let rest for 5 minutes with the steamer lid opened. Transfer the steamed *muthias* to a serving platter.

To make the seasoning: Heat the oil in a small pan over medium heat. Add the mustard seeds, sesame seeds, and curry leaves and cook until the seeds crackle, 30 to 40 seconds.

Drizzle the seasoning on top of the dumplings. Garnish with the grated coconut and cilantro and serve.

PAIRING SUGGESTIONS

Serve with green chutney for a fresh, herby contrast or** kadhi **(Gujarati yogurt-based curry) for a comforting pairing. A side of** chass **(buttermilk) balances the meal beautifully.

Batata Poha

SAVORY FLATTENED RICE WITH POTATOES, PEANUTS, AND CILANTRO

YIELD: 4 SERVINGS (2 LADLES EACH)

Batata Poha is a comforting Maharashtrian breakfast made with flattened rice (*poha*), earthy potatoes, crunchy peanuts, and a generous sprinkling of lemon and cilantro. This dish is lightly spiced, fragrant with a tempering of mustard seeds, curry leaves, and green chiles, making it the perfect quick-fix breakfast or snack for busy mornings. I love how easily this one-pan dish comes together and how filling it is, without being heavy!

1½ cups medium flattened rice (*poha*)

½ teaspoon turmeric powder

2 teaspoons sugar

2 lemons, juiced, plus more lemon juice to taste

¼ teaspoon asafetida

Kosher salt

¼ cup frozen green peas

2 tablespoons sunflower or canola oil

2 tablespoons raw peanuts

½ teaspoon mustard seeds

½ teaspoon cumin seeds

1 onion, finely chopped

1 sprig curry leaves, finely chopped

2-inch piece fresh ginger, peeled and finely chopped

3 green chiles, finely chopped

1 potato, peeled and diced

1 small bunch cilantro, finely chopped

¾ cup fresh pomegranate kernels, for garnish

½ cup *sev/bhujia*, for garnish

PROTEIN TIP

- Add protein to your breakfast by including sprouts, nuts, seeds, or even a boiled or scrambled egg.

THAWING TIP

- Instead of using a microwave, you can cook the peas in a pressure cooker for two whistles and release the pressure immediately.

Using a large strainer, rinse the flattened rice (*poha*) under cold water and drain any excess water. Transfer the rinsed *poha* to a large bowl; stir in the turmeric, sugar, lemon juice, asafetida, and salt, to taste. Set aside.

Transfer the frozen peas to a bowl and add ½ cup of water and a pinch of salt. Cover the bowl and place in the microwave for 3 to 4 minutes on high. Drain and set aside.

Heat 1 tablespoon of oil in a pan over medium heat. Add the peanuts and roast them on low-medium heat until well roasted, at least 5 minutes. Make sure to roast on low-medium heat so the peanuts roast from the inside out. If the heat is too high, the outsides will darken while the insides remain raw. Set aside.

In a separate pan, heat the remaining 1 tablespoon of oil over medium heat. Stir in the mustard seeds and cumin seeds. Once the seeds have crackled, stir in the onion, curry leaves, ginger, and chiles. Sauté until the onions are tender and translucent.

Stir in the potato, add 2 tablespoons of water, sprinkle in a pinch of salt, and cover the pan. Turn the heat to medium and cook the potatoes until done, 4 to 5 minutes.

Once the potatoes are cooked, gradually stir the *poha* mixture into the onion and potato mixture. Sprinkle in about 3 tablespoons of water and gently stir to combine. Turn the heat to low, cover the pan, and let simmer for 4 to 5 minutes. The *poha* should fluff up.

Turn off the heat and stir in the peas, roasted peanuts, and cilantro. Let rest for 1 minute. Check the salt and sugar for taste. The *poha* should taste sweet, tangy, and spicy. If not, add more salt, sugar, or lemon juice and sprinkle in a little water. Steam on medium heat for another 3 to 4 minutes. Garnish with pomegranate kernels and *sev/bhujia*.

PAIRING SUGGESTIONS

Pair with a hot cup of andrak (ginger) tea or masala chai for a traditional breakfast experience. For a refreshing twist, serve alongside a dollop of chilled yogurt or a tangy cilantro-mint chutney. It also tastes great with a side of freshly cut oranges or apples.

Pudina Semiya Upma

MINT-FLAVORED SAVORY VERMICELLI BREAKFAST

YIELD: 4 SERVINGS

Pudina Semiya Upma is a refreshing twist on the classic South Indian breakfast, infused with the aromatic flavors of fresh mint (*pudina*). This light yet wholesome dish combines roasted vermicelli with a simple tempering of mustard seeds, curry leaves, and green chiles, making it a perfect balance of spice and freshness.

***PUDINA* PASTE**

- 1 onion, finely chopped
- 4 cloves garlic, coarsely chopped
- 1-inch piece fresh ginger, coarsely chopped
- 2 green chiles, coarsely chopped
- ½ cup chopped mint leaves (*pudina*)
- ¼ cup chopped cilantro

- 2 tablespoons ghee
- ½ teaspoon mustard seeds
- ½ teaspoon cumin seeds
- 1 teaspoon white urad dal (split)
- 1 sprig curry leaves, finely chopped
- 2 cups *semiya* (vermicelli)
- Kosher salt

Add all the ingredients for the *pudina* paste into a blender jar along with ¼ cup of water and blend to form a paste. The mixture will not be completely smooth. Set aside.

Heat the ghee in a saucepan over medium heat, add the mustard seeds, cumin seeds, and urad dal and allow the seeds to crackle for a few seconds until the dal turns golden brown and crisp. Stir in the curry leaves and sauté for a few seconds. Stir the *pudina* paste into the ghee mixture and sauté for a few seconds more.

Stir in the *semiya* (vermicelli), salt to taste, and add 1½ cups of water. Cover the pan, turn the heat to low, and cook the *upma* until all the water is completely absorbed and the *semiya* is cooked through. Check the salt and adjust according to taste. Once done, turn off the heat and stir gently. Transfer the *upma* to a serving bowl and serve hot for breakfast.

PAIRING SUGGESTIONS

Serve with a side of coconut chutney, peanut chutney, or a bowl of curd to complete the meal. A steaming cup of filter coffee on the side makes it even more comforting!

Spicy South Indian Bread Upma

A QUICK AND FLAVORFUL SAVORY BREAD STIR-FRY

YIELD: 4 SERVINGS

Bread *upma* is a delicious and easy-to-make South Indian dish that transforms leftover bread into a spicy, tangy, and flavorful *upma*. Tossed with mustard seeds, curry leaves, onions, and a hint of spice, this dish offers up a perfect balance of crunch and softness.

16 slices bread (any leftover bread)

Salted butter, softened, for spreading

1 tablespoon sunflower or canola oil

1 teaspoon mustard seeds

2 onions, thinly sliced

2 green chiles, finely chopped

3 tomatoes, finely chopped

3 sprigs curry leaves, coarsely torn

1 teaspoon turmeric powder

1 teaspoon *sambar* powder

Kosher salt

6 sprigs cilantro, finely chopped

Toast the bread using a toaster or skillet. Spread the softened butter over the toast, then cut it into small cubes. Set aside.

Heat the oil in a large wok over medium heat. Add the mustard seeds and allow them to crackle. Stir in the onions and green chiles. Sauté until the onions are soft and tender. Add the tomatoes, curry leaves, turmeric powder, and *sambar* powder. Stir and cook the tomatoes until they soften.

Finally, add salt, to taste, and the toasted bread cubes. Stir well to combine all the ingredients and stir-fry on medium-high heat for 2 minutes, until well combined. Check the salt level and remember, the butter is already salted.

Turn off the heat and stir in the chopped cilantro. Transfer to a serving bowl and serve warm.

PAIRING SUGGESTIONS

Serve with a side of fresh coconut chutney, a bowl of yogurt, or a hot cup of masala chai. Enjoy as a comforting breakfast or a light evening snack!

Crispy Mushroom and Corn Masala Dosa

SOUTH INDIAN–STYLE SAVORY CREPES

YIELD: 12 TO 15 *DOSAS*

This dish is a delicious twist on the classic South Indian *dosa*. Made with a fermented *idli-dosa* batter, the crispy golden *dosa* is stuffed with a flavorful filling of mushrooms, corn, and aromatic spices. The combination of earthy mushrooms and sweet corn adds a delightful contrast of flavors and textures, making this recipe a must-try!

MUSHROOM CORN MASALA

2 tablespoons ghee

1 sprig curry leaves, coarsely chopped

2 onions, finely chopped

1 green bell pepper, finely chopped

6 cloves garlic, finely chopped

2 tomatoes, finely chopped

14 ounces button mushrooms, sliced

1 cup frozen corn, thawed

1 tablespoon garam masala powder

1 teaspoon *sambar* powder

½ teaspoon Kashmiri red chili powder

Kosher salt

¼ cup finely chopped mint leaves

DOSAS

3¾ cups *dosa* batter

Ghee, for cooking

PANTRY TIP

- *Dosa* batter is available at specialty Indian stores.

Heat the ghee in a pan over medium heat. Add the curry leaves and fry for 5 to 10 seconds until fragrant. Add the onions, bell pepper, and garlic and sauté until the onions and bell pepper are soft and tender, 4 to 5 minutes. Add the tomatoes and cook until the tomatoes turn a little mushy. Add the mushrooms and sauté for a few seconds. Cover and cook until the mushrooms wilt down, 3 to 4 minutes.

Once the mushrooms have wilted, add the thawed corn, garam masala, *sambar* powder, red chili powder, and salt, to taste. Stir well until the masala thickens, about 5 minutes. Once done, stir in the chopped mint leaves and turn off the heat.

To make the *dosas*: Heat a flat, nonstick skillet over medium heat. Once the pan is hot, drizzle 1 teaspoon of ghee on the bottom, then spread 1 ladleful of *dosa* batter in the pan. Cook until crisp. Repeat until all the batter is used.

Once the *dosa* is cooked and crisped, place a spoonful of the mushroom corn masala in the center and fold the *dosa* in half. Repeat until all the *dosa* are filled, then serve hot.

PAIRING SUGGESTIONS

Pair with coconut chutney and tomato chutney. Enjoy with a dollop of butter or ghee for an extra-indulgent taste!

Soft and Fluffy Rava Idli

SOUTH INDIAN–STYLE STEAMED SEMOLINA CAKES

YIELD: 12 *RAVA IDLIS*

Rava idli is a classic South Indian breakfast dish that is light, fluffy, and incredibly easy to make. Originating from Karnataka, unlike traditional *idlis* that require fermentation, *rava idli* is an instant version made with semolina (*rava*), yogurt, and a tempering of mustard seeds, curry leaves, and green chiles. These steamed semolina cakes are soft, mildly spiced, and packed with flavor. You will need an *idli* steamer for this recipe.

- 1 teaspoon sunflower or canola oil, plus extra for greasing
- 1 teaspoon mustard seeds
- 1 teaspoon white urad dal (split)
- 1 sprig curry leaves, torn
- 1-inch piece fresh ginger, peeled and grated
- 2 green chiles, finely chopped
- 2 tablespoons chopped cashews
- ¼ teaspoon asafetida
- 1 cup fine semolina (*sooji/rava*)
- 1 cup plain yogurt
- Kosher salt
- 2 sprigs cilantro, finely chopped
- 1 carrot, peeled and grated
- ¼ teaspoon baking soda

Heat the oil in a pan over medium heat; add the mustard seeds and the urad dal and cook until the seeds crackle and the dal turns golden brown and crisp. Stir in the torn curry leaves, grated ginger, green chiles, cashews, and asafetida. Roast for 2 to 3 minutes.

Add the semolina *(rava)* and roast until you get a good aroma, about 1 minute. This is the *rava idli* mixture. Set aside to cool.

Once cooled, in a mixing bowl, combine the roasted *rava idli* mixture along with the yogurt. Add just enough water, about ¼ cup, to make a thick batter. Set aside to rest for 10 to 15 minutes.

In the meantime, preheat an *idli* steamer, adding 2 to 3 cups of water to the reservoir, or enough to cover the bottom by 1 to 1½ inches.

After the resting period, to add a little more water, about ¼ cup, as the *rava idli* batter will have soaked up all the moisture. Add the grated carrot and baking soda and whisk. If the batter is too thick, add more water to make it of dropping consistency. Stir well for about 2 minutes.

Grease the *idli* molds with oil and spoon the batter into the cavities. Place the molds in the preheated steamer and steam on high heat for 10 minutes.

The *rava idli* are cooked when a toothpick inserted comes out clean. Turn off the heat, and spoon them into a serving bowl and serve warm.

PAIRING SUGGESTIONS

Serve with a side of coconut chutney or raw mango chutney or add a dollop of ghee on top for an extra indulgence!

Instant Godhuma Dosa

SOUTH INDIAN–STYLE SAVORY WHOLE WHEAT CREPES

YIELD: 8 TO 10 *DOSAS*

Unlike traditional *dosas*, which require hours of soaking and fermenting, these crispy crepes don't need fermentation. Made with whole wheat flour (*atta*), rice flour, and spices, they are ready in minutes, making them a great, healthy meal for when you're short on time.

1 cup whole wheat flour

½ cup rice flour

1 onion, finely chopped

2 green chiles, finely chopped

1-inch piece fresh ginger, peeled and finely chopped

1 sprig curry leaves, finely chopped

¼ teaspoon asafetida

1 teaspoon whole black peppercorns, coarsely pounded in a mortar and pestle

Kosher salt

Sunflower or canola oil, for cooking

COOKING TIP

- For extra-crispy *dosas*, cook them over medium heat in a cast-iron skillet. Iron skillets maintain heat and produce perfectly textured crepes.

In a large mixing bowl, combine the whole wheat flour, rice flour, onion, green chiles, ginger, curry leaves, asafetida, black pepper, and salt, to taste.

Stir in 2 cups of water to make a lump-free batter. The batter should be of pouring consistency and not very thick. It should be thinner than regular *dosa* or pancake batter.

Heat a skillet over high heat. Pour a ladleful of batter from the outer edges toward the inner into the skillet. The batter will spread automatically with the heat from the pan. It will sizzle to spread itself out. Drizzle 1 teaspoon of oil around the edges and toward the insides.

Cook on both sides, until the edges are browned and slightly crispy. Once done, remove from the skillet. Repeat until all the batter is used. Serve hot.

PAIRING SUGGESTIONS

Serve with coconut chutney, spicy tomato chutney, or a comforting bowl of sambar. Add a side of filtered coffee for the ultimate breakfast experience!

Spiced Besan Cheela with Onions

SAVORY GRAM FLOUR ONION PANCAKES

YIELD: 8 TO 10 *CHEELA*

Besan cheela, a popular North Indian dish, is a quick and protein-packed savory pancake made with gram flour (*besan*), onions, and spices. It's a go-to breakfast or light meal, loved for its crispy edges and soft center. This vegan and gluten-free dish is flavorful, filling, and comes together in minutes!

BATTER

1 cup gram flour

1 onion, finely chopped

2 green chiles, finely chopped

1 teaspoon fennel seeds, coarsely pounded in a mortar and pestle

6 sprigs cilantro, finely chopped

Kosher salt

Sunflower or canola oil, for cooking

FOR SERVING

2 onions, thinly sliced

1 teaspoon chaat masala powder

¼ teaspoon red chili powder

In a large mixing bowl, combine all the ingredients for the *cheela* batter except the oil. Gradually add 1 cup of water to create a thick batter, thick enough to coat the back of a spoon. Check the salt and spice levels and adjust to suit your taste.

Preheat a skillet over medium heat.

Pour a ladleful of batter into the pan and spread it in a circular motion to form a thin crepe (*cheela*). Drizzle 1 teaspoon of oil around the *cheela* and cook it until the edges are getting brown. Flip and cook on the other side for a few seconds. Transfer to a plate and repeat until all the batter is used.

To serve, place a small pinch of the spiced, thinly sliced onions in the center of rach hot *cheela*, then fold it in half, or serve the spiced onions on the side. Serve the *cheelas* hot.

PAIRING SUGGESTIONS

Serve with Green Chutney (page 164) or a bowl of creamy curd for a wholesome meal. Pair with masala chai for a comforting breakfast.

CHAPTER 2

APPETIZERS

Crispy Onion Pakoras

CRISPY ONION FRITTERS

YIELD: 15 TO 20 *PAKORAS*

There's nothing quite as comforting as biting into a plate of piping hot onion *pakoras*, especially on a cold winter day with a hot cup of chai in hand. These crispy, golden fritters are made with thinly sliced onions, spicy chickpea-flour batter, and a touch of love. They are crunchy on the outside, tender inside, and bursting with flavors of ajwain (carom seeds), green chiles, and cilantro. Whether for an evening snack or a festive gathering, these *pakoras* are always a crowd-pleaser.

1 cup gram flour (*besan*)

¼ cup rice flour

3 onions, thinly sliced

10 sprigs cilantro, finely chopped

2 green chiles, finely chopped

1-inch piece fresh ginger, peeled and grated

½ teaspoon turmeric powder

½ teaspoon red chili powder

½ teaspoon ajwain

¼ teaspoon asafetida powder

¼ teaspoon baking soda

Kosher salt

Sunflower or canola oil, for deep frying

Chaat masala powder, for sprinkling

In a large mixing bowl, add the *besan*, rice flour, onions, cilantro, green chiles, ginger, turmeric powder, red chili powder, ajwain, asafetida, baking soda, and salt, to taste, Combine well.

Add very little water, ½ to ¾ cup, to make a thick batter. Check the salt and spice and adjust to suit your taste.

Heat the oil in a deep-frying pan over medium heat. Spoon a portion of the onion *pakora* mixture into the hot oil and allow it to cook until browned and crisp on both sides. Flip it around so it cooks evenly on all sides. Repeat with the remaining batter.

Once done, place the *pakoras* on paper towels to drain excess oil. Arrange them on a platter and sprinkle chaat masala powder over the top.

PAIRING SUGGESTIONS

Serve with Green Chutney (Page 164), Tamarind Chutney (page 166), or even a bowl of hot tomato soup, for a hearty twist.

Kolkata Beet Chop

KOLKATA-STYLE SPICED BEET CUTLETS

YIELD: 12 TO 15 CUTLETS

This vibrant Kolkata Beet Chop is a delightful snack from West Bengal, where grated, spiced beet and mashed potato are formed into cutlets and shallow-fried to perfection. With its gorgeous hue and balanced flavors, it's a reminder of the traditional Bengali chaat culture and makes for an eye-catching treat.

ROASTED SPICES

½ teaspoon fennel seeds

½ teaspoon cumin seeds

2 cardamom pods

2 dried red chiles

½-inch cinnamon stick

½ teaspoon whole black peppercorns

1 teaspoon *kalonji* (onion seeds)

1 carrot

2 beets

1 potato

1 tablespoon roasted peanuts, coarsely pounded in a mortar and pestle

2 green chiles, finely chopped

1-inch piece fresh ginger, peeled and grated

Kosher salt

1 teaspoon sugar

1 cup breadcrumbs (optional)

2 tablespoons cornstarch

Sunflower or canola oil, for frying

10 sprigs cilantro, finely chopped, for garnish

¼ cup chutney (mint or tamarind)

¼ cup ketchup

Heat a pan and roast the dry spices until they pop and release aromatic flavors (fennel, cumin, cardamom, cinnamon, dry red chile, black peppercorn, and *kalonji*). Let cool, then blend to make a smooth powder. Set aside.

Peel the carrot and beets, wash them well, and cut into big chunks. Steam using a steamer or cook in a multi-cooker. Once cooked, allow it to cool and grate. Set aside.

Similarly, boil the potatoes in water or in a multi-cooker. Peel the skin, mash, and set aside.

In a bowl, combine the carrot, beets, potato, green chiles, and ginger. Add the roasted spice powder, salt, to taste, sugar, cornstarch and, if needed, a few tablespoons of breadcrumbs to bind the mixture. Mix well to combine and check the salt and flavors. Shape the mixture into oval shaped cutlets.

Heat the oil in a pan and shallow-fry the cutlets until golden on both sides. Drain on paper towels, garnish with cilantro. Serve with your favorite chutney and ketchup.

Hara Bhara Kebab

PUNJABI-STYLE GREEN VEGGIE KEBABS

YIELD: 12 TO 15 KEBABS

Hara Bhara Kebab is a nutritious snack bursting with the goodness of spinach, green peas, and aromatic herbs. Originating in North India, these kebabs are light yet satisfying and remind me of the vibrant, healthy recipes of Punjabi cuisine—perfect as an appetizer or a midday snack.

2 cups raw spinach, blanched and finely chopped

1 cup frozen green peas, blanched

¼ cup finely chopped cilantro

¼ cup finely chopped fresh mint

2 green chiles, finely chopped

4 cloves garlic, finely chopped

1-inch piece fresh ginger, peeled and finely chopped

2 potatoes, peeled, boiled, and mashed

1 small onion, finely chopped

1 teaspoon fennel seeds, roasted and pounded in a mortar and pestle

2 tablespoons cornstarch

Kosher salt

Freshly ground black pepper

½ teaspoon garam masala

1 teaspoon chaat masala powder

Sunflower or canola oil, for frying

TIPS

- Blanch the spinach lightly to keep its bright color and smooth texture.
- Avoid overmixing to retain a pleasantly coarse bite.

In a large bowl, blend the spinach, peas, cilantro, mint, green chiles, garlic, and ginger to form a coarse mixture. Stir in the mashed potatoes and onion. Next, stir in the fennel seeds, cornstarch, salt and pepper, to taste, garam masala, and chaat masala powder. Combine well and adjust the salt and spices to taste. Shape the mixture into small, flat patties.

Heat the oil in a pan and shallow-fry the kebabs until crisp and golden. Drain on paper towels and serve hot.

PAIRING SUGGESTIONS

Serve with Green Chutney (page 164) along with freshly sliced raw onion and a squeeze of lemon to make a perfect appetizer.

Dahi Vada

CREAMY YOGURT-SOAKED LENTIL DUMPLINGS

YIELD: 15 TO 20 *DAHI VADAS*

Dahi Vada is a refreshing North Indian snack featuring soft, spiced lentil dumplings soaked in thick, creamy yogurt and drizzled with sweet-tangy chutneys. This cooling dish is a festive favorite, offering a delightful mix of textures and flavors that remind me of family celebrations and cozy gatherings.

1 cup whole white urad dal, soaked for 3 hours

2 green chiles, chopped

1-inch piece fresh ginger, peeled and finely chopped

Kosher salt

Sunflower or canola oil, for deep frying

YOGURT SAUCE

2 cups thick plain yogurt

1 teaspoon chaat masala

½ teaspoon red chili powder

½ teaspoon cumin powder

1 teaspoon sugar

Kosher salt

FOR SERVING

½ cup tamarind chutney

½ cup green chutney

1 teaspoon roasted cumin powder

¼ cup chopped cilantro, for garnish

Drain the soaked white urad dal, then add it into the blender along with the green chiles, ginger, and salt, to taste, to make a smooth batter.

Heat the oil in a deep-frying pan and drop spoonfuls of batter to form *vadas*. Fry until golden and crisp.

Heat about 2 liters of water in a large, wide pan and bring it to a boil. Turn off the heat.

Soak the hot *vadas* in the warm water for about 1 hour. The *vadas* will fluff up in the water and become soft and juicy. Gently press the *vadas* to drain out any excess water.

In the meantime, to make the yogurt sauce, in a bowl, whisk the yogurt, chaat masala, red chili powder, cumin powder, sugar, and salt, to taste. Set aside.

Arrange the *vadas* in a serving bowl, then pour the whisked yogurt over them.

When ready to serve, spoon 2 *vadas* into individual serving bowls, drizzle with tamarind and mint-coriander chutneys, and sprinkle roasted cumin powder on top. Garnish with cilantro and serve chilled.

Rajma Galouti Kebab

SPICED KIDNEY-BEAN PATTIES

YIELD: 12 TO 15 KEBABS

Rajma Galouti Kebab reimagines the classic kebab using mashed kidney beans blended with aromatic spices to create incredibly soft patties. Emerging from the regal kitchens of Lucknow, these kebabs are famed for their melt-in-the-mouth texture and subtle, complex flavors—perfect for a refined starter.

½ cup kidney beans (*rajma*), soaked for 8 hours

Kosher salt

2 potatoes

KEBABS

¼ cup finely chopped mint leaves

2 green chiles, chopped

1-inch piece fresh ginger, peeled and finely chopped

3 cloves garlic, chopped

¼ cup cashews (whole or broken)

½ cup grated paneer

1 teaspoon rose water

¼ teaspoon saffron strands

1 teaspoon garam masala powder

1 teaspoon chaat masala powder

2 tablespoons gram flour

Sunflower or canola oil, for cooking

TIPS

- Let the spices meld into the mash before forming patties.
- Fry the kebabs gently to retain a soft interior while achieving a slight crisp on the outside.
- Use the *ramja* water in stocks or soups or even for cooking rice.

Boil the soaked *rajma* along with salt, to taste, until very soft. If you press the *rajma* between your fingers it should mash easily. Once the *rajma* is cooked through completely, drain any excess water.

In the meantime, boil the potatoes until fully cooked, 10 to 15 minutes. Cool, peel, and mash. Set aside.

To make the kebabs: Blend the mint leaves, green chiles, ginger, garlic, and cashews together in a food processor to form a coarse mixture. Add the *rajma* and blend again into a smooth mixture.

In a large mixing bowl, add the remaining kebab ingredients, except the oil, and knead well to make a kebab dough. Adjust the salt and seasoning according to taste. Divide the mixture into 12 to 15 equal portions and shape them into disks.

Preheat a pan and grease it with oil. Place the kebabs on the preheated skillet. Drizzle on a few drops of oil and pan-fry them on both sides until lightly crisp. You may need to work in batches so as not to overcrowd the pan. Place the finished kebabs on a serving platter and serve hot.

PAIRING SUGGESTIONS

Serve with Green Chutney (page 164), sliced raw onions, and lemon wedges for a satisfying appetizer.

Gujarati Dabeli

SPICED POTATO BURGER

YIELD: 4 *DABELIS*

Gujarati Dabeli is a vibrant Gujarat street snack with spiced mashed potatoes in a buttered bun, topped with pomegranate, crunchy *sev*, and tangy chutneys—a sweet, spicy, tangy bite that evokes Ahmedabad's lively stalls.

GARLIC CHUTNEY

¼ cup garlic

1 tablespoon sesame seeds

1 teaspoon cumin seeds

¼ cup desiccated coconut

1 tablespoon Kashmiri red chili powder

1 lemon, juiced

Kosher salt

***DABELI* MASALA**

1 teaspoon fennel seeds

2 tablespoons coriander seeds

1 teaspoon cumin seeds

1 teaspoon sesame seeds

4 dried red chiles

1 teaspoon whole black peppercorns

1-inch piece cinnamon stick

1 brown cardamom

1 star anise pod

¼ cup desiccated coconut

2 teaspoons sugar

1 tablespoon *amchur*

1 teaspoon Kashmiri red chili powder

***DABELI* FILLING**

4 tablespoons butter

4 potatoes, boiled, peeled, and mashed

2 tablespoons tamarind chutney

¼ cup halved roasted peanuts

Kosher salt

DABELI

4 *pav* buns

Salted butter, for spreading

1 onion, finely chopped

½ cup *sev*

½ cup fresh pomegranate kernels

¼ cup finely chopped cilantro

To make the garlic chutney: Blend all the ingredients into a coarse, crumbly mixture. Set aside.

To make the *dabeli* masala: Preheat a pan over medium heat. Roast all the ingredients—fennel seeds, coriander seeds, cumin seeds, sesame seeds, red chile, peppercorns, cinnamon, cardamom, and star anise. Roast for a few seconds until you can smell the aromas coming through and the seeds are popping.

Add the roasted spices to a blender jar and make a fine powder. Add the coconut, sugar, *amchur* powder, and red chili powder and blend to combine. The *dabeli* masala powder is now ready.

To make the *dabeli* filling: Heat the butter in a pan over medium heat. Add the *dabeli* masala and sauté for a few seconds. Add the mashed potatoes, tamarind chutney, and roasted peanuts and sauté until well combined, about 3 to 4 minutes. Check the taste and spices and adjust accordingly. Set aside.

To make the *dabeli*: Slice the *pav* buns in half horizontally. Spread with butter and toast them on the pan on both sides, until the surface is lightly golden and crisp. Turn off the heat and place the buns on a platter.

Smear the garlic chutney on the bottom half of each bun. Spread a large dollop of the *dabeli* filling on the lower half; sprinkle the chopped onion, *sev*, pomegranate, and cilantro on top of the filling; top with the other half of the bun and serve.

PAIRING SUGGESTIONS

Enjoy with a side of Green Chutney (page 164), sweet Tamarind Chutney (page 166), and a hot cup of masala chai for the ultimate street-food experience.

Tandoori Gobi Tikka

GRILLED CAULIFLOWER TIKKA

YIELD: 6 TO 8 SERVINGS

Tandoori Gobi Tikka is a delectable vegetarian appetizer from North India where cauliflower florets are marinated in a spiced yogurt mixture and then grilled to smoky perfection. This dish's vibrant colors and bold flavors make it a party favorite and a must-try for any barbecue enthusiast.

1 head cauliflower, cut into large florets

1 cup plain *hung* curd (Greek yogurt)

4 cloves garlic, finely chopped

½ teaspoon red chili powder

1 teaspoon garam masala powder

1 teaspoon chaat masala powder

½ teaspoon turmeric powder

1 teaspoon coriander powder

½ teaspoon ajwain

1 teaspoon *kasuri methi* (dried fenugreek leaves)

3 tablespoons gram flour

Kosher salt

Sunflower or canola oil, for cooking

2-inch piece of coal, if using the coal-smoking method

1 teaspoon ghee (optional)

TIPS

- Preheat the grill or wok to ensure a good char on the florets.
- Steaming the cauliflower helps it absorb the tikka masala.
- Turn the florets occasionally for even cooking.

Steam the cauliflower on high heat for about 4 minutes, until it is just about cooked but still firm. Transfer the steamed cauliflower to a large mixing bowl. Add the *hung* curd, garlic, red chili powder, garam masala powder, chaat masala powder, turmeric powder, coriander powder, ajwain, *kasuri methi*, gram flour, and salt, to taste. Stir well. Cover and let marinate for at least 30 minutes.

Once the marinating is done, cook the tikkas using one of the following methods.

To barbecue: Prepare a charcoal barbecue.

In the meantime, thread the florets onto wooden skewers. If using wooden skewers, soak them in water for at least 30 minutes prior to threading to prevent them from burning on the grill. Once the barbecue is ready, grill the skewers on both sides, applying a little oil until they turn brown and charred marks.

To cook in a wok: Heat the oil in a wok over medium heat; add the marinated cauliflower pieces, and stir-fry for 2 to 3 minutes.

Meanwhile, prepare the coal for the coal-smoking method. Heat a small piece of charcoal until red-hot. Place it in a small steel bowl and set inside the wok with the cauliflower. Pour the ghee over the hot charcoal and cover the wok with a lid. Infuse for 2 to 3 minutes—this gives an authentic, smoky tandoori aroma.

Transfer the grilled Tandoori Gobi Tikka to a platter and serve.

PAIRING SUGGESTIONS

Serve with Green Chutney (page 164), thinly sliced raw onions or pickled onions, and lemon wedges. It's also excellent when paired with naan, a favorite dal, and a curry.

Mutton Shami Kebab

MELT-IN-YOUR-MOUTH MUTTON PATTIES

YIELD: 10 TO 15 KEBABS

A royal treat from Mughlai cuisine, Mutton Shami Kebabs are made with finely minced mutton blended with lentils and spices. Their melt-in-your-mouth texture and rich aroma make them a nostalgic favorite of North Indian feasts.

2 tablespoons ghee

4 dried red chiles

1 teaspoon ajwain

1 teaspoon fennel seeds

5 cardamom pods

1 tablespoon whole black peppercorns

4 cloves

1-inch piece cinnamon stick

1 onion, finely chopped

10 cloves garlic, coarsely chopped

1-inch piece fresh ginger, peeled and chopped

2 green chiles, finely chopped

18 ounces boneless mutton, washed

1 cup chana dal (Bengal gram dal), soaked for 2 to 3 hours

½ teaspoon turmeric powder

Kosher salt

½ cup finely chopped mint leaves

In a preheated pressure cooker or multi-cooker, add the ghee, red chiles, ajwain, fennel seeds, cardamom pods, peppercorns, cloves, cinnamon, onion, garlic, ginger, and green chiles. Sauté for a few seconds and then add the mutton. Sear the meat for about 5 minutes, until browned.

Add the chana dal, turmeric powder, salt, to taste, and just enough water to completely immerse the ingredients. Pressure-cook for 5 to 6 whistles, or for about 20 minutes in a multi-cooker. Allow the pressure to release naturally.

If there is any moisture in the pressure cooker, turn on the heat and keep stirring until the moisture has evaporated. Turn off the heat and let the mixture cool.

Attach the chopping blade to a food processor. Add the cooled *shami* kebab mixture to the jar and grind into a coarse paste. Once done, add the mint leaves. Pulse to combine well.

Transfer the pulsed kebab mixture into a bowl and shape into small, flat patties.

Shallow-fry in hot oil over medium heat until golden on both sides and cooked through, 4 to 5 minutes per side. Drain on paper towels and serve hot with your favorite chutneys.

PAIRING SUGGESTIONS

Serve with Green Chutney (page 164) or Tamarind Chutney (page 166), sliced raw onions, and parathas, as an appetizer on their own.

Hariyali Chicken Tikka

CORIANDER-MINT CHICKEN TIKKA

YIELD: 10 TO 12 KEBABS

This refreshing twist on classic chicken tikka uses a vibrant marinade of coriander and mint blended with yogurt and spices. A North Indian favorite, its tangy, herbaceous flavor makes it ideal for festive feasts and family get-togethers.

1 cup finely chopped cilantro, plus more for garnish

1 cup fresh mint leaves, chopped

¼ cup plain yogurt

2-inch piece fresh ginger, peeled and chopped

6 cloves garlic, chopped

2 green chiles, chopped

1 teaspoon red chili powder

½ teaspoon turmeric powder

1 teaspoon garam masala

Kosher salt

1 tablespoon lemon juice

2 tablespoons sunflower or canola oil, plus more for frying

18 ounces boneless chicken, cut into cubes

In a blender jar, add the cilantro, mint, yogurt, ginger, garlic, green chiles, red chili powder, turmeric, garam masala, salt, to taste, lemon juice, and 2 tablespoons of oil and blend into a smooth marinade.

Toss the chicken cubes in the marinade, cover, and refrigerate for at least 2 hours.

Heat oil in a nonstick pan. Shallow-fry the marinated chicken on high heat until the underside turns a deep golden color. Flip and cook the other side on high heat until golden, 10 to 15 minutes.

Alternatively, thread the marinated chicken onto skewers and broil or bake them in an oven set at 400°F for 25 to 30 minutes, until cooked through and lightly charred. Garnish with cilantro and serve.

PAIRING SUGGESTIONS

Pair with Green Chutney (page 164), sliced raw onions, and lemon wedges and serve as an appetizer for a party or weekend brunch.

Chicken Galouti Kebab

DELICATE MINCED-CHICKEN KEBABS

YIELD: 10 TO 15 KEBABS

A tribute to the famed Lucknowi Galouti Kebabs, these Chicken Galouti Kebabs are exceptionally tender and richly spiced. The fine mince and aromatic spices create a luxurious, melt-in-your-mouth texture that elevates any meal.

1 tablespoon sunflower or canola oil

1 onion, sliced

½ teaspoon kabab *chini* (optional)

18 ounces chicken breast, chopped

6 cloves garlic, chopped

1-inch piece fresh ginger, peeled and chopped

½ teaspoon garam masala powder

4 cardamom pods

1 teaspoon rose water

Handful of saffron strands

A few drops of *mughlai meetha attar* (optional)

1 teaspoon red chili powder

½ teaspoon coriander powder

¼ cup gram flour

Kosher salt

Ghee, for frying

Heat the oil in a preheated pan over medium heat. Add the sliced onion and sauté until caramelized. Turn off the heat and let cool. Set aside.

Pound the kebab *chini*, if using, in a mortar and pestle to create a fine powder. Set aside.

Add the chopping blade to a food processor, then add the chicken. Blend to make a smooth mince.

Add the caramelized onion, garlic, ginger, garam masala powder, cardamom, rose water, saffron strands, *mughlai meetha attar* (if using), kabab *chini* powder (if using), chili powder, coriander powder, gram flour, and salt, to taste, to the minced chicken. Blend to combine all the ingredients. Remove the mixture to a bowl. Cover and refrigerate for 2 hours.

After 2 hours, divide and shape the mixture into round kebabs.

Heat the ghee in a pan over medium heat and shallow-fry the kebabs for 4 to 5 minutes per side, until cooked and lightly charred on both sides. Drain on paper towels and serve hot.

PAIRING SUGGESTIONS

Pair with Green Chutney (page 164), sliced onions, and lemon wedges, and serve as an appetizer for a party or a weekend brunch.

Kerala-Style Mutton Pepper Fry

SPICY, PEPPERY MUTTON STIR-FRY

YIELD: 4 TO 5 SERVINGS

A fiery delight from the backwaters of Kerala, this Mutton Pepper Fry is loaded with tender mutton pieces stir-fried with black pepper, curry leaves, and spices. Its intense heat and robust flavors are a testament to authentic South Indian coastal cuisine.

18 ounces mutton, cut into pieces

PASTE

2-inch piece fresh ginger, peeled and chopped

8 cloves garlic

2 green chiles

2 tablespoons freshly ground black pepper

1 teaspoon red chili powder

½ teaspoon turmeric powder

Kosher salt

2 tablespoons coconut oil

2 onions, thinly sliced

2 sprigs curry leaves, coarsely torn

2 green chiles, slit

Cilantro, for garnish

Wash, then pat dry the mutton with paper towels. Set aside.

Into a blender, add the ginger, garlic, and green chiles to make a paste. If needed, add 1 to 2 tablespoons of water to achieve a smooth consistency.

Combine the ginger-garlic paste, black pepper, red chili powder, turmeric, and salt, to taste. Rub on the mutton and marinate for at least 2 hours.

Heat the coconut oil in a heavy-bottomed pan, then add the onions and curry leaves and sauté over medium heat until golden. Add the marinated mutton and green chiles and ½ cup of water. Stir-fry on medium heat until the mutton is tender, the oil separates, and the water is evaporated, 30 to 40 minutes. Cover the pan to fasten the cooking process. Once done, transfer to a serving platter. Garnish with cilantro and serve hot.

PAIRING SUGGESTIONS

Serve with steamed rice or a light Tamil Nadu-Style Coconut Chutney (page 167) to balance the spice.

Mutton Ghee Roast

RICH AND SPICY GHEE-ROASTED MUTTON

YIELD: 4 TO 5 SERVINGS

A signature dish from the Konkani/Goan kitchens, Mutton Ghee Roast features succulent mutton slow roasted in generous ghee and an aromatic blend of spices. Intensely flavorful and slightly spicy, it's a celebration of coastal culinary traditions that never fails to impress.

18 ounces mutton, cut into pieces

MARINADE

½ cup plain yogurt

½ teaspoon turmeric powder

1 tablespoon lemon juice

Kosher salt

GHEE ROAST MASALA

6 dried red chiles

1 teaspoon whole black peppercorns

2 cloves

1 teaspoon *methi* seeds (fenugreek seeds)

2 teaspoons coriander seeds

1 teaspoon cumin seeds

6 cloves garlic

1 tablespoon tamarind paste

2 tablespoons ghee

2 sprigs curry leaves

2 teaspoons jaggery

Kosher salt

To marinate the mutton: In a mixing bowl, combine the mutton, along with the yogurt, turmeric powder, lemon juice, and salt, to taste. Mix well and massage the marinade into the mutton pieces. Set aside for a minimum of 30 minutes, or even overnight.

To make the ghee roast masala: Heat a skillet over medium heat. Add the red chiles, peppercorns, cloves, *methi* seeds, coriander seeds, and cumin seeds. Dry roast for 4 to 6 minutes, or until the aroma of the spices wafts in the air. Turn off the heat and let cool.

In a blender jar, blend the roasted spices, garlic cloves, and tamarind paste into a smooth paste. Add 1 tablespoon of water, if needed. Transfer the ghee roast masala into a bowl and set aside.

To make the Mutton Ghee Roast: In a pressure cooker or electric multi-cooker, add the marinated mutton with ¼ cup of water and close the lid. Pressure-cook for 3 to 4 whistles, or until the mutton is about 80 percent cooked. Turn off the heat and allow the pressure to release naturally. Set aside.

Heat the ghee in a wok over medium heat. Once the ghee is hot, add the curry leaves.

When the curry leaves splutter, add the freshly ground ghee roast masala, and cook until the ghee comes up to the surface. This will take 4 to 6 minutes.

To the ghee roast masala, add the cooked mutton along with the stock from the pressure cooker. The roast should be a thick coating consistency, so do not add too much of the stock unless you are looking to make a gravy dish. Add the jaggery and adjust the salt.

Cover and cook the Mutton Ghee Roast for 8 to 10 minutes over low heat. Turn off the heat once done. Check the salt and spices and adjust according to taste. Transfer to a serving bowl and serve hot.

PAIRING SUGGESTIONS

Serve with steamed rice or bhakri and a side of cooling cucumber raita.

CHAPTER 3

SABZI—EVERYDAY VEGETABLES

Aloo Methi Sabzi

SPICED POTATO AND FENUGREEK STIR-FRY

YIELD: 4 SERVINGS

A classic comfort dish from North India, Aloo Methi Sabzi combines soft potatoes with aromatic fresh fenugreek (*methi*) leaves. Its earthy, slightly bitter *methi* perfectly complements the tender potatoes—a staple in Punjabi kitchens that brings back warm memories of home cooking.

2 tablespoons sunflower or canola oil

2 cups chopped *methi* leaves (fenugreek leaves)

Kosher salt

1 teaspoon cumin seeds

2 onions, thinly sliced

1-inch piece fresh ginger, peeled and finely chopped

4 cloves garlic, finely chopped

18 ounces baby potatoes, boiled and peeled

1 bay leaf, torn in half

1-inch cinnamon stick, broken

½ teaspoon turmeric powder

¼ teaspoon red chili powder

1 teaspoon *amchur* (dry mango powder)

½ teaspoon coriander powder

½ teaspoon garam masala powder

Heat 1 tablespoon of oil in a saucepan over medium heat; add the chopped *methi* leaves and sauté until they become soft and wilt down. Sprinkle with salt, to taste. Set aside.

In a separate pan, heat the remaining 1 tablespoon of oil over medium heat; add the cumin seeds and cook until they crackle. Add the onions, ginger, and garlic and sauté until the onions are soft and tender. Add the boiled and peeled potatoes, bay leaf, cinnamon stick, turmeric powder, red chili powder, *amchur*, coriander powder, garam masala powder, and salt, to taste. Stir well to combine and turn the heat to low. Roast the potatoes and spices for 10 minutes, more if needed.

Once the potatoes have absorbed all the spices, add the sautéed *methi* leaves and stir-fry for 30 seconds to 1 minute to combine. Taste and adjust the spices accordingly. Once done, turn off the heat and transfer to a serving bowl. Serve hot.

Sweet Potato and Broccoli Sabzi

SWEET POTATO AND BROCCOLI STIR-FRY

YIELD: 4 SERVINGS

Sweet Potato and Broccoli Sabzi is a flavorful dish inspired by modern Indian cuisine, blending nutrient-rich sweet potatoes and vibrant broccoli with traditional spices. This sabzi beautifully combines health and taste, making it an excellent choice for everyday meals.

The natural sweetness of sweet potatoes complements the earthy flavors of broccoli, whereas spices like cumin, turmeric, and red chili powder enhance the dish with a delightful aroma and a hint of heat. It's a perfect way to include seasonal vegetables in your diet, with a modern twist.

1 tablespoon sunflower or canola oil

1 head broccoli, cut into florets

Kosher salt

½ teaspoon cumin powder

½ teaspoon cumin seeds

1 sweet potato, peeled and cut lengthwise

1 teaspoon red chili powder

1 teaspoon turmeric powder

Heat the oil in a skillet over medium heat. Add the broccoli, then sprinkle with cumin powder and salt, to taste.

Cover and cook the broccoli until it is almost done, 4 to 6 minutes. Once done, transfer to a bowl and set aside.

Heat the oil in a stir-fry pan over medium heat. Add the cumin seeds and cook until they sizzle. Add the sliced sweet potato, salt, to taste, red chili powder, and turmeric powder. Stir to combine, cover the pan, and cook until the potato is cooked through, about 10 minutes.

Add the steamed broccoli florets to the pan and stir to combine. Stir-fry for 1 minute. Turn off the heat and serve warm.

Bhindi Tamatar Ki Sabzi

SPICED OKRA WITH TOMATOES

YIELD: 4 SERVINGS

Bhindi Tamatar Ki Sabzi is a cherished North Indian dish where fresh okra is sautéed with onions, tomatoes, and a blend of aromatic spices. Its tangy and robust flavor evokes memories of festive family dinners and traditional *dhaba* fare.

2 tablespoons sunflower or canola oil

1 teaspoon ajwain

1 onion, thinly sliced

14 ounces bhindi (okra), cut into 1-inch pieces

Kosher salt

2 tomatoes, finely chopped

½ teaspoon turmeric powder

1 teaspoon red chili powder

1 teaspoon coriander powder

6 sprigs cilantro, finely chopped

COOKING TIP

- To prevent the slime in okra, ensure it's completely dry before cutting and cooking. When you cook, keep the lid ajar, allowing some moisture to escape.

Heat the oil in a heavy-bottomed pan over medium heat. Add the ajwain and onion and sauté until tender. Once tender, add the okra and salt, to taste.

Cover the pan with its lid ajar and cook, stirring occasionally, until the okra is tender, at least 10 minutes. Once tender, add the tomatoes. The tomatoes will release their liquid, causing the bhindi to turn mushy; keep the lid open so the excess moisture evaporates.

Once the tomatoes are soft; stir in the turmeric powder, red chili powder, coriander powder, and, if needed, more salt.

Stir well until all the ingredients are well combined, then sauté for another 3 to 4 minutes. Check the salt and seasonings and adjust according to taste. Transfer to a serving dish, stir in the chopped coriander leaves, and serve hot.

Begun Bhaja

BENGALI-STYLE SPICED FRIED-EGGPLANT SLICES

YIELD: 4 SERVINGS

A much-loved vegetable from Bengal, Begun Bhaja features thin slices of eggplant that are spiced and deep-fried to a perfect crisp. Its smoky, caramelized edges and tender interior remind me of nostalgic Bengali street-food treats.

Kosher salt

1 *begun* (eggplant), sliced into ½-inch disks

Gram flour, for dusting (optional)

1 teaspoon red chili powder

1 teaspoon turmeric powder

1 teaspoon garam masala powder

1 teaspoon *amchur* (dry mango powder)

Mustard oil, for frying

Sprinkle salt over the eggplant slices and let them sit for 10 minutes, then pat dry thoroughly with paper towels. Dust lightly with gram flour for extra crispness, if using.

In a bowl, combine the red chili powder, turmeric, garam masala powder, *amchur* powder, salt, to taste, and mix well.

Place a skillet over medium heat and add the mustard oil. It is important to heat the mustard oil until it gets smoky, as that produces maximum flavor.

When the oil begins to smoke, reduce the heat to low and add the eggplant slices to the pan, arranging them in a single layer. Increase the heat to low-medium and fry for 3 to 4 minutes on one side before flipping to cook on the other side and frying for 3 to 4 minutes more. Cook until sufficiently golden on both sides.

Remove the slices individually using a slotted spoon, drain on paper towels, and serve immediately while still hot.

Jaipuri Aloo Pyaz Ki Sabzi

JAIPUR-STYLE POTATO AND ONION STIR-FRY

YIELD: 4 SERVINGS

This rustic sabzi from Jaipur combines tender potatoes and sweet onions simmered with aromatic spices in a pressure cooker. Its bold flavors and homey warmth reflect the traditional Rajasthani palate and evoke memories of hearty homestyle cooking.

18 ounces baby potatoes (or regular potatoes)

2 tablespoons mustard oil, for cooking

1 bay leaf, coarsely torn

6 cloves garlic, finely chopped

1-inch piece fresh ginger, finely chopped

2 green chiles, slit

9 ounces pearl onions

Kosher salt

½ cup homemade tomato purée

2 tablespoons plain yogurt

½ teaspoon turmeric powder

1½ teaspoons Kashmiri red chili powder

1 teaspoon coriander powder

1 teaspoon garam masala powder

6 sprigs cilantro, finely chopped

Preheat a pressure cooker over medium heat.

Pressure-cook the potatoes in water until firmly cooked, about 15 minutes. Peel and set aside.

In a wok, add the mustard oil, bay leaf, garlic, ginger, green chiles, and pearl onions, and sauté until the onions have softened and lightly browned. Stir in the potatoes, sprinkle with salt, to taste, and roast the potatoes for 5 to 6 minutes.

Once done, add the tomato purée, yogurt, turmeric powder, chili powder, coriander powder, garam masala, and salt, to taste. Stir well to combine and sauté for another 15 minutes, until a semi-thick gravy forms.

Check the salt and seasoning and adjust according to taste. Stir in the cilantro. Transfer to a serving bowl and serve hot.

Carrot Bean Thoran

KERALA-STYLE CARROT AND BEAN STIR-FRY

YIELD: 4 SERVINGS

A festive and yet a very homey dish from Kerala, Carrot Bean Thoran features carrots and green beans stir-fried with freshly grated coconut and a tempering of mustard seeds. Its vibrant flavors and crunchy texture bring to mind joyful Onam celebrations and family feasts.

3 carrots, peeled and finely chopped

1 cup green beans, finely chopped

Kosher salt

***THORAN* MASALA**

½ cup fresh, grated coconut

2 green chiles, coarsely chopped

1 teaspoon cumin seeds

1 teaspoon coconut oil (or other vegetable oil)

½ teaspoon mustard seeds

1 teaspoon white urad dal (split)

2 sprigs curry leaves, coarsely chopped

¼ cup pearl onions, finely chopped

½ teaspoon turmeric powder

In a pressure cooker, add the carrots and green beans, salt, to taste, and 2 tablespoons water. Pressure-cook for 2 whistles, or 5 minutes. Turn off the heat. Release the pressure immediately to avoid discoloration of the vegetables and produce a firm yet cooked texture. Set aside.

To make the *thoran* masala: Into a mixer grinder, add the coconut, green chiles, and cumin seeds and blend into a coarse mixture. Set aside.

Heat the oil in a wok over medium heat; add the mustard seeds and urad dal and cook until the dal crackles and turns a light golden brown. Stir in the curry leaves and sauté for a few seconds.

Add the onions and sauté them over medium heat until they turn soft and translucent. Add the turmeric powder and the ground *thoran* masala. Sauté for a few seconds. Stir in the steamed carrots and beans. Check the salt and adjust according to taste. Stir for 1 minute and turn off the heat. Transfer to a serving bowl and serve hot.

Baingan Bharta

SPICY SMOKY-EGGPLANT MASH

YIELD: 4 SERVINGS

Baingan Bharta is a soulful North-Indian dish where eggplant is charred to perfection, then mashed and simmered with tomatoes, green chiles, and spices. Its deep, smoky flavor and velvety texture evoke cherished memories of leisurely family meals.

2 eggplants (*baingan*); yields about 2 cups roasted eggplant, or *brinjal*

1 tablespoon sunflower or canola oil

1 teaspoon cumin seeds

1-inch piece fresh ginger, peeled and finely chopped

6 cloves garlic, finely chopped

3 green chiles, finely chopped

2 onions, thinly sliced

1 bay leaf, torn

1-inch piece cinnamon stick

2 tomatoes, finely chopped

¼ teaspoon turmeric powder

1 teaspoon Kashmiri red chili powder

1 teaspoon coriander powder

¼ teaspoon cumin powder

Kosher salt

2 tablespoons ghee

6 sprigs cilantro, finely chopped

Preheat the oven to 350°F.

Place the whole eggplant on a baking sheet and bake for 30 minutes, or until it has started to soften and the outer skin is charred. The eggplant is ready when a knife can be inserted easily into the flesh. If the flesh is not tender, continue baking for 20 minutes more, or until done.

Alternatively, roast the eggplant on the stovetop: Place the *brinjal* on the open stovetop flame. Use tongs to turn it while roasting, and monitor continuously. After about 10 minutes, the skin will begin to char and the insides will become tender. To test, insert a knife into the flesh; if it is hard, continue to roast until tender, about 5 minutes more.

Allow the *brinjal* to cool. Peel the charred skin and discard. Finely mince the pulp.

Heat the oil in a pan over medium-high heat; add the cumin seeds and cook until they crackle. Add the ginger, garlic, green chiles, onions, bay leaf, and cinnamon, and sauté until the onions soften. Add the tomatoes, turmeric powder, red chili powder, coriander powder, cumin powder, and sauté until the tomatoes are soft and tender. Stir in the roasted *brinjal*, salt, to taste, and ghee. Combine well.

Turn the heat to low and simmer for 5 minutes, until the flavors of the *brinjal*, tomatoes, and spices meld. Turn off the heat, stir in the cilantro, and serve hot.

Karwar-Style Bibya Usal

SPICED CASHEW STIR-FRY

YIELD: 4 SERVINGS

Hailing from the Konkan region near Karwar, this innovative sabzi features cashews simmered in a tangy, spiced gravy. Its rich, robust flavor and delightful crunch offer a unique twist to traditional coastal cuisine—a favorite of adventurous eaters.

1 cup whole cashews
1 tablespoon coconut oil
½ teaspoon mustard seeds
1 teaspoon white urad dal (split)
2 dried red chiles, halved
2 green chiles, finely chopped
1-inch piece fresh ginger, peeled and finely chopped
4 cloves garlic, finely chopped
1 sprig curry leaves, torn
¼ cup freshly grated coconut
1 teaspoon sugar
¼ teaspoon turmeric powder
Kosher salt
1 lemon, juiced
6 sprigs cilantro, finely chopped

Soak the cashews in warm water for 15 minutes. Drain and set aside.

Heat the oil in a heavy-bottomed pan over medium heat. Add the mustard seeds and urad dal and let the seeds crackle and the dal turn golden brown and crisp. Add the red chiles, green chiles, ginger, and garlic. Sauté for a few seconds.

Add the soaked cashews, curry leaves, coconut, sugar, and turmeric powder and toss to combine. Add 2 to 3 tablespoons water and salt, to taste. Keep sautéing for 2 minutes over medium heat, or until all the water from the cashews is evaporated and absorbed.

Check the salt and adjust to taste. Turn off the heat and stir in the lemon juice and cilantro. Transfer to a serving bowl and serve hot.

Arbi Shimla Mirch Sabzi

COLOCASIA AND BELL-PEPPER STIR-FRY

YIELD: 4 SERVINGS

Arbi Shimla Mirch Sabzi is a soulful dish from North Indian kitchens, especially popular in Punjabi households. It beautifully marries tender *arbi* (taro root) with crisp, vibrant bell peppers (*simla mirchi*), all simmered in an aromatic blend of spices. Every time I cook this sabzi, I'm taken back to warm family gatherings, where its rich, comforting flavors would bring everyone together around the table.

10 ounces taro root (*arbi*)

2 tablespoons sunflower or canola oil

1 teaspoon ajwain

1-inch piece fresh ginger, peeled and finely chopped

1 green bell pepper, diced

1 tomato, finely chopped

½ teaspoon turmeric powder

Kosher salt

1 teaspoon coriander powder

1 teaspoon garam masala powder

½ teaspoon red chili powder

6 sprigs cilantro, finely chopped

In a pressure cooker or electric multi-cooker, add the taro root and ½ cup water. Pressure-cook on high heat for 4 to 5 whistles, or 5 minutes in an electric multi-cooker. Turn off the heat.

Let the pressure release naturally, then peel and dice the taro root and set aside. Let cool completely.

Heat the oil in a heavy-bottomed saucepan; add the ajwain and allow it to crackle. Stir in the ginger and bell pepper. Sauté for 2 to 3 minutes, until the bell pepper has softened. Add in the tomato, turmeric powder, and salt, to taste, and keep sautéing until the tomatoes become mushy.

At this point, stir in the cooked *arbi*, coriander powder, garam masala powder, red chili powder, and more salt, to taste. Simmer for 5 to 8 minutes, until the *arbi* is well coated. Turn off the heat, stir in the cilantro. Transfer to a serving bowl and serve hot.

Kathirikai Poondu Pirattal

GARLIC EGGPLANT STIR-FRY

YIELD: 4 SERVINGS

A rustic South Indian delight, Kathirikai Poondu Pirattal features tender eggplant cubes stir-fried with a generous amount of garlic and spices. Hailing from Tamil Nadu, its robust, aromatic flavors make it a standout dish for any homestyle meal.

18 ounces long green eggplant (about 5 eggplants)

2 tablespoons sunflower or canola oil

1 teaspoon mustard seeds

1 teaspoon white urad dal (split)

¼ teaspoon asafetida

1 sprig curry leaves

1 dried red chile, halved

12 cloves garlic, chopped

1 onion, finely chopped

2 tomatoes, finely chopped

½ teaspoon turmeric powder

1 tablespoon *sambar* powder

Kosher salt

Chop the eggplants lengthwise and place them in a bowl filled with salted water at room temperature until you are ready to cook.

Heat the oil in a pan over medium heat; add the mustard seeds and urad dal. Heat until the seeds crackle and the dal turns golden brown and crisp. Stir in the asafetida, curry leaves, and red chile; cook for about 10 seconds.

Next, add the garlic and onion and fry until the onions become soft, about 1 minute. Stir in the tomatoes and turmeric powder and sauté until the tomatoes have softened. Drain the eggplant from the water, season with salt, to taste, and give it a stir.

Cover the pan and cook on low-medium heat for 10 to 15 minutes, until softened. Stir in the *sambar* powder. Stir-fry for another 4 to 5 minutes, until the flavors are well incorporated. Check the salt and adjust according to taste. Transfer to a serving bowl and serve hot.

Kerala-Style Avial

MIXED VEGETABLE AND COCONUT MEDLEY

YIELD: 4 SERVINGS

A celebrated dish from Kerala, Avial is a medley of seasonal vegetables simmered in a mildly spiced coconut and yogurt gravy. Its fresh, earthy flavors evoke memories of festive Onam feasts and the comforting warmth of coastal cuisine.

1 cup peeled and chopped ash gourd (also called winter melon)

2 moringa drumsticks, cut into 1-inch pieces

2 carrots, peeled and julienned

10 green beans, julienned

1 banana, peeled and julienned

2 potatoes, peeled and julienned

1 cup peeled and julienned elephant foot yam

½ teaspoon turmeric powder

Kosher salt

COCONUT GRAVY

1½ cups freshly grated coconut (or frozen and thawed)

3 green chiles, chopped

1 teaspoon cumin seeds

1 tablespoon coconut oil

2 tablespoons plain yogurt

1 sprig curry leaves, torn

In a pressure cooker, add the ash gourd, moringa, carrots, green beans, banana, potatoes, yam, and turmeric. Pressure-cook over high heat for 2 whistles, or 5 minutes. Turn off the heat. Set aside.

To make the coconut gravy: Place the coconut, green chiles, and cumin seeds in a blender jar. Add ½ cup of warm water and blend to an almost smooth consistency.

Add the coconut gravy to the vegetable and fruit mixture, then add the coconut oil, yogurt, and curry leaf and stir well. Adjust the salt, to taste, and serve warm.

Keerai Thoran

STIR-FRIED AMARANTHUS LEAVES WITH COCONUT

YIELD: 4 SERVINGS

Keerai Thoran is a wholesome Kerala classic featuring amaranth leaves quickly stir-fried with grated coconut, mustard seeds, and curry leaves. Its earthy, comforting flavor and vibrant green color make it a nutritious side that reminds me of simple, healthy family meals in South India.

½ cup fresh coconut

1 tablespoon cumin seeds

1 tablespoon whole black peppercorns

Kosher salt

1 teaspoon coconut oil

½ teaspoon mustard seeds

1 teaspoon white urad dal (split)

2 sprigs curry leaves, roughly torn

2 cups red amaranth leaves (or spinach leaves), finely chopped

In the small jar of the mixer grinder, add the coconut, cumin seeds, black peppercorns, and salt, to taste. Blend to make a coarse, dry mixture.

Preheat the oil in pan over medium heat. Add the mustard seeds and urad dal and cook until the seeds crackle and the dal turns golden brown. Stir in the curry leaves, the amaranth leaves, and salt, to taste. Stir-fry the greens until they wilt and are cooked, about 10 minutes.

Stir in the ground coconut mixture. Sauté for about 2 minutes, so all the flavors meld. Check the salt and adjust according to taste. Transfer to a serving bowl and serve warm.

CHAPTER 4

DALS AND LEGUMES

Dal Tadka

LEMON-AND-CORIANDER-INFUSED DAL

YIELD: 4 SERVINGS

A classic favorite, Dal Tadka is transformed by a zesty infusion of lemon and cilantro. This dish from North India is simple yet bursting with vibrant flavors that brighten even the dullest day—comfort in a bowl!

1 cup yellow *moong* dal (split), rinsed

½ teaspoon turmeric powder

1-inch piece fresh ginger, peeled and grated

2 green chiles, finely chopped

1 bay leaf, torn

Kosher salt

SEASONING

1 teaspoon ghee

½ teaspoon cumin seeds

¼ teaspoon asafetida

1 lemon, juiced

4 sprigs cilantro, finely chopped

In a pressure cooker or electric multi-cooker, add the *moong* dal, turmeric powder, ginger, green chiles, bay leaf, 2½ cups of water, and salt, to taste. Pressure-cook for 2 to 3 whistles, or 10 minutes, if using an electric multi-cooker. Allow the pressure to release naturally. Whisk the dal until it reaches a semi-smooth texture.

To make the seasoning: Heat the ghee in a saucepan; add the cumin seeds and cook until they crackle. Stir in the asafetida and pour in the cooked dal. Bring to a brisk boil. Add salt, to taste, Turn off the heat, add the lemon juice, and stir in the cilantro. Transfer to a serving bowl and serve hot.

Creamy Dhaba-Style Dal Makhani

DHABA-STYLE CREAMY LENTILS

YIELD: 4 SERVINGS

Dal Makhani is a legendary dish from Punjabi cuisine, known for its creamy texture, smoky flavor, and rich, buttery taste. Traditionally slow-cooked for hours, this *dhaba*-style version brings out the deep, earthy flavors of the whole black lentils (urad dal) and kidney beans (*rajma*), which are simmered with tomatoes, butter, and aromatic spices.

This comforting dish is a staple at roadside *dhabas* across North India, where it's cooked overnight on charcoal for that signature depth of flavor. The combination of slow-cooking, butter, and a final touch of cream gives it an irresistible, velvety texture.

2 to 3 tablespoons ghee

1 teaspoon cumin seeds

1-inch piece fresh ginger, peeled and finely chopped

4 cloves garlic, finely chopped

2 green chiles, finely chopped

1 bay leaf, torn

1-inch piece cinnamon stick, halved

1 tomato, finely chopped

½ teaspoon turmeric powder

½ teaspoon cumin powder

1 teaspoon red chili powder

½ teaspoon garam masala powder

¼ teaspoon cardamom powder

1 cup whole black lentils (urad dal), soaked overnight

Kosher salt

¼ cup fresh cream

1 tablespoon *kasuri methi* (dried fenugreek leaves)

2-inch piece of charcoal, for smoking (optional)

6 sprigs cilantro, finely chopped

TIPS

- Let the dish infuse for at least 1 minute using the *dhungar* method for a smoky, *dhaba*-style aroma; the charcoal can be washed and reused.
- Pressure-cooking (or using an electric multi-cooker) quickly yields the soft, creamy texture of traditional Punjabi dal, which is typically simmered for hours for deeper richness.

Heat the ghee in a pressure cooker over medium heat; add the cumin seeds and cook until they crackle. Add the ginger, garlic, and green chiles and sauté for about 5 seconds. Add the bay leaf, cinnamon stick, tomatoes, turmeric powder, cumin powder, red chili powder, garam masala powder, and cardamom powder. Sauté on medium heat until the tomatoes soften, about 5 minutes.

Add the soaked dal and kidney beans, soaking water included, to the pressure cooker. Top off with water until the dal-*rajma* mixture is covered by 2 inches of water. Add salt, to taste. Pressure-cook for 35 to 40 minutes; turn off the heat and allow the pressure to release naturally. If using an electric multi-cooker, set the valve to sealing and cook on high for 40 minutes. Use the natural pressure release (NPR) and let stand for 15 minutes. The dal should be cooked well so that when pressed against the fingers it should mash up.

Heat the ghee in a heavy-bottomed pan; add the cooked dal *makhani*, cream, and *kasuri methi*. Turn the heat to low, add about ¼ cup of water, and simmer for 10 to 15 minutes. While simmering, keep mashing the dal so it becomes creamy and stir to keep it from sticking.

To smoke (optional): Heat the charcoal over a stovetop flame for about 5 minutes, until it develops red-hot spots. Place a small bowl in the center of the dal *makhani* pan and put the hot coal inside. Add a few drops of ghee, which will begin to smoke. Cover the pan; after about 1 minute, open the lid and remove the bowl. You will notice a delicious smoky flavor.

Transfer to a serving bowl, stir the cilantro, and serve hot.

Gujarati Dal

SWEET AND SPICY LENTILS

YIELD: 4 SERVINGS

This Gujarati dal is a delightful balance of sweet, tangy, and spicy notes that transforms simple lentils into a comforting dish. It's a personal favorite for its lively flavors and satisfying finish.

1 cup split *toor dal* (split pigeon pea lentils)

1-inch piece fresh ginger, peeled and finely chopped

2 green chiles, finely chopped

1 bay leaf (*tej patta*), torn

½ teaspoon turmeric powder

½ teaspoon red chili powder

1 tomato, finely chopped

2 tablespoons jaggery

1-inch piece cinnamon stick (*dalchini*), broken

2 tablespoons raw peanuts

Kosher salt

1 tablespoon ghee

½ teaspoon mustard seeds

½ teaspoon cumin seeds

1 sprig curry leaves, torn

1 lemon, juiced

6 sprigs cilantro, finely chopped

In a pressure cooker or electric multi-cooker, add the *toor dal*, ginger, green chiles, bay leaf, turmeric powder, red chili powder, tomato, jaggery, cinnamon stick, peanuts, 2½ cups of water, and the salt, to taste. Cook for 3 whistles, turn the heat to low, and simmer for 5 to 7 minutes. Turn off the heat. Let the pressure release naturally, as the dal will continue to cook. If using an electric multi-cooker, cook for 15 minutes.

While the *toor dal* is still hot, whisk until it blends to a smooth, soupy texture with no lumps. Use a hand blender or a potato masher to mash well until smooth.

In a preheated saucepan, add the ghee, mustard and cumin seeds and cook until the seeds crackle. Stir in the curry leaves and sauté for a few seconds. Add the dal and bring to a brisk boil, then turn the heat to low and simmer for 5 to 10 minutes. Check the salt and spices and adjust to taste. Add the lemon juice. Transfer to a serving bowl, stir in the cilantro, and serve hot.

Gujarati Khatta Mag

GREEN MUNG BEAN IN BUTTERMILK CURRY

YIELD: 4 SERVINGS

Hailing from Gujarat, this tangy and refreshing curry uses green *moong* dal simmered in buttermilk with a blend of sweet and sour spices. It's a light, cooling dish that recalls the vibrant flavors of Gujarati *thalis* and is perfect for a summer meal.

½ cup whole green *moong* dal, soaked for 30 minutes

½ cup plain yogurt

2 tablespoons gram flour (*besan*)

¼ teaspoon turmeric powder

Kosher salt

¼ teaspoon asafetida

1 teaspoon sunflower or canola oil

½ teaspoon mustard seeds

½ teaspoon cumin seeds

1 sprig curry leaves, coarsely torn

2 green chiles, finely chopped

1 teaspoon finely chopped fresh ginger

4 tablespoons cilantro, finely chopped, for garnish

In a pressure cooker or electric multi-cooker, cook the green *moong* dal in 2 cups of water for 10 minutes over medium heat, until soft and tender but not mushy.

Whisk in the yogurt, gram flour, turmeric powder, salt, to taste asafetida, and 1 cup of water until smooth. Set aside.

Heat the oil in a pan over medium heat; add the mustard seeds, cumin seeds, and curry leaves and cook until the seeds crackle, 20 to 30 seconds. Add the green chiles and ginger, and sauté for 30 seconds. Stir in the yogurt and green *moong* mixture. Bring to a boil, then turn the heat to low. Simmer for 5 minutes. Check the salt and adjust according to taste.

Divide among 4 bowls, garnish each with 1 tablespoon of cilantro, and serve hot.

Chettinad Poondu Rasam

SPICE AND TANGY GARLIC SOUP

YIELD: 4 SERVINGS

This fiery Chettinad *rasam* is a burst of bold flavors—infused with garlic, tamarind, and a secret blend of spices. It's a signature South Indian soup that always brings warmth on a chilly day, reminiscent of my own childhood in Tamil Nadu.

¼ cup split *toor dal* (split pigeon peas)

¾ ounce tamarind, soaked in hot water for 15 minutes

1 tablespoon ghee

½ teaspoon mustard seeds

½ teaspoon cumin seeds

¼ teaspoon asafetida

2 sprigs curry leaves, coarsely chopped

6 cloves garlic, peeled and crushed

3 tomatoes, chopped and puréed

½ teaspoon turmeric powder

1 teaspoon red chili powder

½ teaspoon black pepper powder

½ teaspoon cumin powder

1½ teaspoons coriander powder

1 teaspoon sugar

Kosher salt

6 sprigs cilantro, finely chopped, for garnish

Cook the *toor dal* in 1 cup of water in a pressure cooker or electric multi-cooker for 15 minutes over medium heat. Allow the pressure to release naturally. Once the pressure releases, whisk the dal to give it a smooth texture.

Extract the pulp from the soaked tamarind to produce 1 cup of tamarind water. Set aside.

Heat the ghee in a saucepan over medium heat. Add the mustard seeds and cumin seeds. Allow them to crackle. Add the asafetida, curry leaves, and garlic, and sauté for a few seconds, until the aromas of garlic come through.

Add the tomato purée, cooked dal, tamarind water, turmeric powder, red chili powder, black pepper powder, cumin powder, coriander powder, sugar, and salt, to taste. Stir well. Add 1 cup of water or more if required to get a flowing consistency of the *rasam*.

Turn the heat to medium-high and bring a brisk boil. Turn the heat to medium-low and simmer for 10 minutes. The *rasam* will begin to froth up around the edges. This is a good indication that it is cooked and has all its flavors. Check the salt and spices and adjust to taste accordingly. Stir in the cilantro, transfer to a serving bowl, and serve hot.

PAIRING SUGGESTIONS

Serve with Sweet Potato and Broccoli Sabzi (page 58), Kerala-Style Avial (page 72), steamed rice, Hesarukalu Bele Kosambari (page 145), and Coorg Mange Pajji (page 161).

Arachuvitta Sambar

SOUTH INDIAN LENTIL CURRY WITH FRESHLY GROUND SPICES

YIELD: 4 SERVINGS

This hearty South Indian *sambar* is enriched with a freshly ground spice mix (*arachuvitta*), lending it a vibrant tang and depth of flavor. It's a soulful dish that always reminds me of comforting meals in Tamil Nadu, perfect for a rainy day.

1 cup split *toor dal* (pigeon peas)

1 large tamarind, soaked in hot water for 10 minutes

ROASTED AND GROUND SPICES

1 tablespoon chana dal (Bengal gram dal)

1 tablespoon white urad dal (split)

2 tablespoons coriander seeds

1 teaspoon *methi* seeds (fenugreek seeds)

4 dried red chiles

¼ cup fresh coconut, grated

1 carrot, peeled and diced

1 radish, peeled and diced

1 moringa, cut into 1-inch pieces

1 tomato, diced

½ cup pearl onions, quartered

1 teaspoon turmeric powder

Kosher salt

***TADKA* SEASONING**

1 teaspoon oil

¼ teaspoon mustard seeds

2 sprigs curry leaves, torn roughly

2 dried red chiles, broken into half

¼ teaspoon asafetida

6 sprigs cilantro, finely chopped

Pressure-cook the *toor* dal over medium heat in 2 cups of water for 10 minutes. Allow the pressure to release naturally. Whisk the dal until smooth. Set aside.

Extract the water from the tamarind pulp twice to yield 2 cups of extract. Set aside.

To make the roasted spices: In a small skillet, add the Bengal gram dal and the urad dal; roast on medium heat until the dal is well roasted and has turned golden brown. Do not brown too quickly. Add the coriander seeds, *methi* seeds, and red chiles and roast for 1 minute. Add the grated coconut and roast until the aroma comes through. Turn off the heat. Allow the roasted sambar spice mixture to cool a bit. Once cooled, grind the mixture in a mixer grinder to make a powder. Set aside.

To prepare the vegetables: In a pressure cooker, add the prepared tamarind extract, carrot, radish, moringa, tomato, onions, turmeric powder, salt, to taste, and the ground *sambar* powder. Pressure-cook for 2 whistles, about 5 minutes, and turn off the heat.

Add the cooked dal into the tamarind water. Stir well to combine. Check the salt and adjust to suit your taste. Boil briskly for 2 minutes. Adjust the consistency by adding water, if needed, and simmer for 2 to 3 minutes more.

To make the tadka for the *sambar:* Heat the oil in a small pan over medium heat. Add the mustard seeds, curry leaves, red chiles and allow them to crackle. Finally, add the asafetida powder to the oil and stir. Turn off the heat. Add this *tadka* to the *sambar*, stir in the chopped cilantro, and transfer to a serving bowl. Serve hot.

Kerala Kadala Curry

SPICY CHICKPEAS IN COCONUT GRAVY

YIELD: 4 SERVINGS

A staple from the coastal kitchens of Kerala, Kerala Kadala Curry is a robust chickpea curry simmered in a fragrant coconut gravy. Its rich, spicy, and creamy taste brings the authentic flavors of South India to your table, reminiscent of festive feasts and family gatherings.

COCONUT PASTE

1 cup fresh coconut

1 teaspoon fennel seeds

2 tablespoons coriander seeds

1 cup *kala* chana (brown chickpeas), soaked overnight

Kosher salt

1 tablespoon coconut oil

½ teaspoon mustard seeds

15 pearl onions, finely chopped

5 cloves garlic, finely chopped

1-inch piece fresh ginger, peeled and finely chopped

2 green chiles, slit

2 sprigs curry leaves, finely chopped

2 tomatoes, chopped and puréed

¼ teaspoon turmeric powder

½ teaspoon red chili powder

To make the coconut paste: In a mixer grinder jar, add the coconut, fennel seeds, and coriander seeds. Add ½ cup of warm water and blend to make a smooth paste.

Place the soaked chickpeas in a pressure cooker or electric multi-cooker along with salt, to taste, and 2½ cups of water. Cook for 30 to 40 minutes. Allow the pressure to release naturally.

Heat the oil in a heavy-bottomed pan over medium heat. Add the mustard seeds and cook until they crackle. Add the onions, garlic, ginger, and green chiles and sauté until the onions are soft and translucent. Add the curry leaves and sauté for a few seconds more. Stir in the tomato purée, turmeric powder, red chili powder, and the coconut purée and stir well.

Add the cooked chickpeas and salt, to taste, and bring to a boil. Add 1 cup of water, stir well, and turn the heat to low. Simmer for 15 minutes, until all the masala is well absorbed. Taste and adjust the salt and red chili powder accordingly. Transfer to a serving bowl and serve hot.

PAIRING SUGGESTIONS

Serve with Keerai Thoran (page 73), Arbi Shimla Mirch Sabzi (page 68), Tawa Paratha (page 128), steamed rice, and Beet Raita (page 154).

Amritsari Chole Masala

SPICED CHICKPEA CURRY

YIELD: 4 SERVINGS

This classic Amritsari Chole Masala is a robust chickpea curry steeped in the rich flavors of Punjab. Its deep, spiced gravy and tender chickpeas bring back memories of bustling *dhabas* and festive family feasts.

2 cups white chickpeas (*kabuli* chana), soaked overnight

1 teaspoon kosher salt, plus more as needed

AMRITSARI *CHOLE* MASALA POWDER

2 tablespoons coriander seeds

2 teaspoons cumin seeds

1-inch piece cinnamon stick

4 cloves

1 brown cardamom (*badi elaichi*)

2 tablespoons dried *anardana* seeds (pomegranate seeds)

2 tablespoons whole black peppercorns

2 teaspoons Kashmiri red chili powder

1 teaspoon *amchur* (dry mango powder)

3 tablespoons ghee

1 onion, thinly sliced

2-inch piece fresh ginger, finely chopped

4 cloves garlic, finely chopped

2 green chiles, finely chopped

1 tomato, finely chopped

½ teaspoon turmeric powder

1 teaspoon black salt (*kala namak*)

6 sprigs cilantro, chopped, for garnish

2-inch piece fresh ginger, julienned

Add the chickpeas and 1 teaspoon salt to the pressure cooker or electric multi-cooker. Ensure the water covers the chickpeas by at least 2 inches. Pressure-cook for 45 minutes. Once done, turn off the cooker and allow the pressure to release naturally.

In the meantime, to make the amritsari chole masala powder: Preheat a skillet over medium heat; add the coriander seeds, cumin seeds, cinnamon, cloves, *badi elaichi*, *anardana* seeds, and black peppercorns. Roast on medium-high heat for 5 minutes, until you get a roasted aroma and the spices turn a roasted color. Stir to ensure they roast evenly. Turn off the heat and let cool.

Once cooled, add the roasted chole masala spices into the small jar of a mixer grinder. Add the Kashmiri red chili powder and *amchur* powder, and blend to make smooth powder. Set aside.

Add the ghee to a preheated pan over medium heat; add the onion, ginger, garlic, green chiles, and sauté until the onion softens. Add the tomato and sauté until the tomato softens. Add the dry amritsari *chole* masala, turmeric powder, and *kala namak* and sauté for a few seconds. Stir in the cooked chickpeas and combine well.

Cover the pan and simmer for 30 minutes. The masala will attain a thick, gravy consistency. Mash a few chickpeas to make it a thick gravy, if required. Check the salt and add more, if required. Turn off the heat and stir in the cilantro. Transfer to a serving bowl and serve hot with julienned ginger.

Punjabi Rajma Masala

HEARTY KIDNEY-BEAN CURRY

YIELD: 4 SERVINGS

A robust and hearty dish from Punjab, this Rajma Masala is prepared in a single pot for convenience without compromising on flavor. The tender kidney beans simmer in a spiced tomato gravy that warms the soul and brings back memories of lively family dinners.

1 teaspoon sunflower or canola oil

1 onion, finely chopped

1-inch piece fresh ginger, peeled and finely chopped

3 cloves garlic, finely chopped

1 green chile, finely chopped

1 tomato, finely chopped

1 bay leaf, torn

1-inch piece cinnamon stick, halved

¼ teaspoon turmeric powder

2 teaspoons cumin powder

½ teaspoon red chili powder

1 teaspoon garam masala powder

Kosher salt

2 cups *rajma* (kidney beans), soaked for 8 hours, or overnight

8 sprigs cilantro, finely chopped

Heat the oil on medium heat in the pressure cooker or electric multi-cooker; add the onion, ginger, garlic, and green chile, and sauté for 3 to 4 minutes, until the onion softens and turns a light golden color. Stir in the tomato, bay leaf, cinnamon stick, turmeric powder, cumin powder, red chili powder, garam masala powder, and salt, to taste. Sauté for 2 to 3 minutes, until the tomatoes become soft and mushy.

Add the soaked *rajma*, along with its water. Add more water, if needed. There should be enough water to cover the *rajma* by at least 2 inches. Cover and cook on medium heat for about 40 minutes. Once done, turn off the heat and allow the pressure cooker to release its pressure naturally.

Check that the *rajma* is ready. If you press the beans between your fingers, they should mash easily.

If they are still firm, cook for about 10 minutes. Check the salt and spice levels, and adjust to suit your taste. Stir in the chopped cilantro and serve hot.

Dhaba-Style Dal Palak

SPINACH LENTIL CURRY

YIELD: 4 SERVINGS

This Dhaba-Style Dal Palak blends wholesome lentils with fresh spinach in a vibrant, spiced gravy. A nourishing Punjabi favorite, it brings a burst of color and nutrition to your table and always reminds me of hearty home-cooked meals.

2 tablespoons ghee

1 onion, finely chopped

2-inch piece fresh ginger, finely chopped

2 green chiles, finely chopped

4 cloves garlic, finely chopped

1 tomato, finely chopped

¼ teaspoon turmeric powder

½ teaspoon garam masala powder

1 cup split *toor* dal (split pigeon peas), washed

Kosher salt

2 dry red chiles, broken

1 teaspoon cumin seeds

2 cups spinach leaves (*palak*), finely chopped

1 lemon, juiced

Heat 1 tablespoon of the ghee in a pressure cooker; add the onion, ginger, green chiles, and garlic and sauté until the onion turns soft. Add the tomato, turmeric powder, and garam masala powder and sauté until the tomato softens.

Add the *toor* dal, salt, to taste, add 2½ cups of water, and cover the pressure cooker. Pressure-cook for 4 to 5 whistles, then turn off the heat. Allow the pressure to release naturally. Once done, whisk the dal to give it a smooth texture.

In the meantime, heat the remaining 1 tablespoon ghee in a saucepan, then add the red chiles and cumin seeds. Stir-fry until the seeds crackle and the red chiles are roasted.

Stir in the chopped spinach and sauté until the spinach wilts. Stir in the cooked dal and bring to a brisk boil. Check the salt and adjust to taste. Add the lemon juice, transfer to a serving bowl, and serve hot.

CHAPTER 5

CURRIES AND GRAVIES

Bagara Baingan

EGGPLANT IN A SPICED PEANUT AND SESAME CURRY

YIELD: 4 SERVINGS

Bagara Baingan is a Hyderabadi specialty that pairs beautifully with biryani and parathas. Also known as Baingan Ka Salan, this rich, nutty curry features baby eggplants cooked in a tangy and mildly spiced gravy made with peanuts, sesame seeds, and coconut. It's a dish I always associate with celebratory meals, where the aroma of toasted spices and caramelized onions fills the kitchen. Every bite is a harmony of flavors—earthy, tangy, and subtly sweet—making it a favorite for those who love deep, layered curries.

PASTE

3 tablespoons sesame seeds

3 tablespoons roasted peanuts

1 small piece of tamarind

¼ cup fresh coconut, grated

1 onion, coarsely chopped

12 cloves garlic

1-inch piece fresh ginger, coarsely chopped

2 green chiles, chopped

4 tablespoons sunflower or canola oil

½ teaspoon mustard seeds

1 bay leaf

1-inch piece cinnamon stick

3 cloves

½ teaspoon turmeric powder

1 teaspoon red chili powder

1 teaspoon coriander powder

Kosher salt

12 small eggplants (*baingan*), about 18 ounces

6 sprigs cilantro, for garnish

ROASTING TIP

- Covering the pan when pan-roasting traps the steam inside and shortens cooking time.

To make the paste: In a heavy-bottomed pan, add the sesame seeds and roast for 1 minute until the sesame seeds start popping. Turn off the heat and let cool. Add the sesame seeds, peanuts, tamarind, coconut, and ½ cup of warm water into a mixer grinder and blend to make a smooth paste. Set aside.

Next, add the onion, garlic, ginger, and green chiles into a mixer grinder and grind well to make a smooth paste. Set aside.

Heat 2 tablespoons of oil in a heavy-bottomed pan over medium heat; add the mustard seeds and cook until they crackle. Add the bay leaf, cinnamon stick, and cloves and sauté for a few seconds until the aromas from the spices come through. Stir in the onion paste and sauté on medium heat for 4 to 5 minutes, until the paste is cooked and starts to change the color.

Add all the ground spice powders, including the turmeric powder, red chili powder, coriander powder, peanut sesame paste, and salt, to taste, and 1 cup of water to adjust the consistency of the gravy. Bring to a boil and boil briskly for 3 to 4 minutes. Turn off the heat and set aside.

Slit the eggplants into quarters without removing the stem. If using large eggplants, cut them lengthwise to 1-inch thickness and about 2 inches in length. Heat 2 tablespoons of oil in a pan and shallow-roast the eggplants with a little salt until tender, cooked, and browned. Optionally, cover the eggplant and pan-roast it.

Add the sautéed *baingan* into the Bagara Baingan gravy and boil until it reaches the desired consistency, about 5 minutes. Check the salt and spices and adjust according to taste. Turn off the heat, transfer the Bagara Baingan to a serving bowl, garnish with cilantro, and serve hot.

Palak Paneer

COTTAGE CHEESE IN SPINACH GRAVY

YIELD: 4 SERVINGS

A North Indian classic, Palak Paneer is a creamy, nutrient-packed dish made with puréed spinach and soft cubes of paneer. The velvety texture of the spinach gravy combined with the richness of the paneer makes this dish a family favorite, perfect for everyday meals and special occasions alike. I remember my grandmother making this dish in winter when fresh spinach was at its best—its vibrant green color and earthy aroma still bring back warm memories!

1 tablespoon ghee
1-inch piece fresh ginger, peeled and finely chopped
3 cloves garlic, finely chopped
2 green chiles, finely chopped
1 tomato, finely chopped
1-inch piece cinnamon stick
¼ teaspoon turmeric powder
18 ounces spinach leaves (*palak*), chopped
1 teaspoon cumin powder
1 teaspoon garam masala powder
1 tablespoon butter
½ teaspoon cumin seeds
1 bay leaf, torn into half
2 tablespoons fresh cream
7 ounces paneer, cubed
Kosher salt

Heat 1 tablespoon ghee in a sauté pan over medium heat; add the ginger, garlic, and green chiles and sauté for a few seconds. Stir in the tomato, cinnamon, and turmeric powder and sauté until the tomato softens.

Next, add the chopped spinach, cumin powder, and garam masala powder. Sauté until the spinach wilts, about 5 minutes. Turn off the heat and set aside to cool. Once cooled, pulse the spinach in a blender to make a smooth mixture.

Melt the butter in a frying pan over medium heat; add the cumin seeds and bay leaf. Sauté the ingredients for a few seconds. Stir in the spinach mixture, cream, and paneer cubes and bring to a brisk boil. Add salt, to taste. Transfer to a serving dish and serve hot.

Kadai Paneer

SPICED COTTAGE CHEESE WITH GREEN BELL PEPPERS

YIELD: 4 SERVINGS

A bold and flavorful dish straight from the heart of North India, *Kadai* Paneer is a must-have in every Indian kitchen. This semidry curry is made with paneer (Indian cottage cheese) and crunchy bell peppers, tossed in a robust blend of freshly ground spices. The name *Kadai* comes from the traditional Indian wok in which the dish is prepared, lending it a smoky, rustic flavor. This is one of those dishes that instantly reminds me of special family dinners and restaurant-style indulgence, but it's surprisingly simple to re-create at home!

2 tablespoons ghee
1 teaspoon cumin seeds
1 onion, diced
1 green bell pepper, diced
1 teaspoon ginger, finely chopped
4 cloves garlic, finely chopped
2 tomatoes, finely chopped
½ teaspoon turmeric powder
1 teaspoon cumin powder
1 teaspoon cardamom powder
1 *badi elaichi* (brown cardamom)
1 teaspoon black pepper powder
1 teaspoon red chili powder
Kosher salt
1 teaspoon sugar
9 ounces paneer, diced
1 tablespoon *kasuri methi* (dried fenugreek leaves)

Heat the ghee in a wok over medium heat. Add the cumin seeds and cook until they crackle. Add the onion, green bell pepper, ginger, and garlic and sauté until the onion and pepper are tender.

Once the onion and pepper have turned slightly tender, add the tomatoes, turmeric powder, cumin powder, cardamom powder, badi *elaichi*, black pepper powder, and red chili powder and sauté until the tomatoes have softened. Stir in the salt, to taste, sugar, paneer pieces, and *kasuri methi*. Cover the pan and simmer the *kadai* paneer for 5 minutes on low heat. Check the salt and spices and adjust according to taste. After a few minutes, turn off the heat. Transfer the *Kadai* Paneer to a serving bowl and serve warm.

Bengali Aloo Dum

SPICED BABY POTATOES IN A TANGY YOGURT GRAVY

YIELD: 4 SERVINGS

Bengali Aloo Dum is a comforting, slightly tangy, and mildly spicy potato curry that is a staple in Bengali households. Made with baby potatoes cooked in a tomato-yogurt gravy, this dish is a beautiful blend of mustard oil, whole spices, and ghee. I love how this dish reminds me of lazy Sunday brunches when it would be paired with soft *luchis* (deep-fried bread), making every bite a melt-in-your-mouth experience.

PASTE

1 onion, coarsely chopped

1-inch piece fresh ginger, peeled and chopped

2 green chiles, chopped

4 cloves garlic

BABY POTATOES

1 tablespoon mustard oil

10 ounces baby potatoes, boiled and peeled

Pinch of turmeric powder

Kosher salt

***DUM* ALOO**

1 tablespoon mustard oil

1-inch piece cinnamon stick

4 cardamom pods

4 cloves

2 bay leaf, torn into half

4 tomatoes, chopped and puréed

1 teaspoon turmeric powder

1 teaspoon coriander powder

1 teaspoon red chili powder

1 teaspoon garam masala powder

½ cup plain yogurt

1 tablespoon sugar

Kosher salt

6 sprigs cilantro, finely chopped

ROASTING TIP

- The process of roasting the potatoes gives an added flavor to the dish, making it healthier and skipping the traditional process of deep-frying the potatoes in oil.

To make the paste: Add the onion, ginger, green chiles, and garlic to a blender jar and grind into a smooth paste. Set aside.

To make the potatoes: Heat 1 tablespoon mustard oil in a frying pan over medium heat. Add the boiled potatoes, turmeric powder, and salt, to taste. Sauté the potatoes until they are light golden-brown in color and slightly crisp. Set aside.

To make the *dum* aloo: In the same frying pan, heat 1 tablespoon of mustard oil. Add the onion paste. Sauté on low heat until the paste turns golden and the raw onion smell disappears, at least 5 minutes. Stir in the cinnamon, cardamom, cloves, and bay leaf. Roast for 2 minutes, until the aroma fills the air.

Next, add the tomato purée, turmeric powder, coriander powder, red chili powder, and garam masala powder. Stir the ingredients until they are well combined. Add the yogurt and mix well.

Next, add in the potatoes and sugar. Check the salt levels and adjust according to taste. Cover the pan and simmer on low heat for about 30 minutes, stirring occasionally.

Once the masala has thickened and coats the potatoes well it indicates that the *dum* aloo is ready. Transfer to a serving dish. Stir in the cilantro and serve hot.

Tirunelveli Mor Kuzhambu

SPICED BUTTERMILK CURRY

YIELD: 4 SERVINGS

A traditional dish from Tamil Nadu, Tirunelveli Mor Kuzhambu is a tangy buttermilk-based curry, flavored with fresh coconut, green chiles, and tempered spices. It's light yet packed with flavor, making it perfect for a hot summer day. I grew up eating this with steamed rice and crispy *vadagams*, a true taste of home!

COCONUT PASTE

2 teaspoons white urad dal (split)

1 teaspoon cumin seeds

¼ teaspoon *methi* seeds (fenugreek seeds)

5 dried red chiles

1 cup fresh coconut, grated

1 ounce tamarind

9 ounces white pumpkin (*vellai poosanikai*), peeled and cubed

Kosher salt

½ teaspoon turmeric powder

2 cups plain yogurt

TADKA

1 teaspoon coconut oil

½ teaspoon mustard seeds

1 teaspoon white urad dal

1 sprig curry leaf, torn

To make the coconut paste: Heat a small frying pan over medium heat; add the urad dal, cumin seeds, *methi* seeds, and red chiles. Roast for 1 minute, until the seeds crackle. Add the coconut and sauté for a few seconds.

Add the roasted ingredients to a blender jar, add ½ cup of warm water, and blend to make a smooth paste. Set aside.

Soak the tamarind in hot water for 10 minutes. Extract the water from the pulp to get 1 cup of tamarind extract. Set aside.

Pressure-cook the white pumpkin with salt, to taste, turmeric powder, and 2 tablespoons of water for 2 whistles. Let the pressure release naturally.

In a saucepan, add the yogurt and whisk well. Add the tamarind water, cooked white pumpkin, the coconut mixture, and salt, to taste. Mix well to combine. Give it a brisk boil *only* when you are ready to eat the curry.

To make the *tadka*: Heat the coconut oil over medium heat in a *tadka* pan. Add the mustard seeds and urad dal and cook until the seeds crackle and the dal turns golden brown. Stir in the curry leaves.

Pour this seasoning over the Tirunelveli Mor Kuzhambu mixture. Once you are ready to have your meal, give this Tirunelveli Mor Kuzhambu a brisk boil for about 2 minutes and turn off the heat.

Transfer to a serving bowl and serve hot.

Kerala Special Vegetable Stew

FRAGRANT COCONUT-MILK CURRY

YIELD: 4 SERVINGS

This mild and creamy vegetable stew is a classic from Kerala's coastal kitchens, where the fragrance of coconut and curry leaves fills the air. The slow-cooked vegetables soak up the rich coconut milk, creating a subtly spiced yet deeply satisfying dish. It reminds me of peaceful mornings in Kerala, where this stew is served with *appams*, making for a light and nourishing meal.

2 potatoes, peeled and diced

10 green beans, cut lengthwise

1 carrot, peeled and diced

9 ounces coconut milk

1 sprig curry leaves, roughly torn

3 cloves

1 teaspoon whole black peppercorns, coarsely pounded in a mortar and pestle

2 or 3 green chiles, slit lengthwise

1 teaspoon sugar

Kosher salt

2 teaspoons coconut oil

VEGETABLE TIP

- This versatile dish tastes delicious with many different vegetables, so add those of your choosing.

FLAVOR TIP

- Allowing the stew to rest after cooking brings out the flavors of the curry leaves, green chiles, and coconut milk.

Steam the potatoes, beans, and carrot for 15 minutes until fork-tender. Set aside.

In a heavy-bottomed saucepan, add the cooked vegetables, coconut milk, curry leaves, cloves, black peppercorns, and green chiles. Stir well and bring the mixture to a brisk boil. Add the sugar and salt, to taste.

Adjust the gravy to get the right consistency by adding about a ¼ cup of water if you want a thinner consistency. However, make sure the gravy is not too watery. Finally, add the coconut oil and simmer for a few more minutes.

Turn off the heat, cover the pan, and let rest for about 10 minutes. Transfer to a serving bowl and serve hot.

Mixed Vegetable Korma

SOUTH INDIAN–STYLE SPICY COCONUT CURRY

YIELD: 4 SERVINGS

A comforting dish from Tamil Nadu and Karnataka, this Mixed Vegetable Korma is an aromatic, creamy curry made with ground coconut, poppy seeds, and spices. Every spoonful brings back childhood memories of Sunday lunches at home, where the fragrance of warm spices and coconut would linger in the air. It's the perfect balance of rich and mildly spiced, making it a great pairing for soft rotis or fragrant pulao.

12 green beans, finely chopped

2 carrots, diced small

1 cup cauliflower, cut into florets

2 potatoes, peeled and diced

KORMA SPICES

1 teaspoon fennel seeds

1-inch piece cinnamon stick

3 cloves

3 cardamom pods

1 teaspoon poppy seeds

COCONUT MASALA

¼ cup fresh coconut, grated

2 green chiles, coarsely chopped

3 cloves garlic

1-inch piece fresh ginger, peeled and chopped

¼ cup mint leaves, finely chopped

1 tablespoon sunflower or canola oil

12 pearl onions, finely chopped (or 1 large onion)

1 tomato, finely chopped

2 bay leaves, torn

½ teaspoon turmeric powder

Kosher salt

To steam the green beans, carrots, cauliflower, and potatoes, place them in a pressure cooker or electric multi-cooker with ¼ cup water and cook for 3 to 5 minutes. Set aside.

To make the korma spices: In a small skillet over medium heat, add the fennel seeds, cinnamon, cloves, cardamom, and poppy seeds. Roast the spices until you can smell the aromas wafting in the air, about 30 to 40 seconds. Let cool. Pound the roasted spices in a mortar and pestle or mix in a spice blender to make a powder. Set aside.

To make the coconut masala: In a blender, add the coconut, green chiles, garlic, ginger, and mint leaves. Add ¼ cup of warm water and blend to make a smooth paste. Transfer to a small bowl and set aside.

Heat 1 tablespoon of oil in a heavy-bottomed pan; add the onions and sauté for 2 minutes, until the onions are tender. Add the chopped tomato and sauté until it softens. Add the ground spice mixture, coconut mixture, bay leaves, and turmeric powder.

Stir in the steamed vegetables. Sauté for 3 to 5 minutes, until the vegetables are coated in the korma mixture. Add 1 cup water. Cover the pan and simmer over medium heat for 5 to 8 minutes, until the mixture thickens. Add salt, to taste. Transfer to a serving dish and serve hot.

Dum Pukht Gosht

SLOW-COOKED MUTTON CURRY

YIELD: 6 SERVINGS

A dish from the royal kitchens of Awadh, Dum Pukht Gosht is a slow-cooked mutton curry where tender meat absorbs rich, aromatic spices over hours of cooking. The term *dum pukht* means "slow-cooking in its own steam," and the process results in a luxurious, melt-in-the-mouth dish. Whenever I make this, I picture a slow-simmering *handi* filled with fragrant spices, just like in the Nawabi era!

2 tablespoons ghee, divided

1 onion, thinly sliced

2 brown cardamom (*badi elaichi*)

2 green cardamom pods

4 cloves

1 teaspoon cumin seeds, divided

1-inch piece cinnamon stick

1 tablespoon whole black peppercorns

8 cloves garlic, divided

2-inch piece ginger, peeled and chopped, divided

4 green chiles, chopped, divided

18 ounces mutton

1½ cups plain yogurt

1 teaspoon red chili powder

1 teaspoon coriander powder

½ teaspoon turmeric powder, divided

½ teaspoon garam masala powder, divided

Kosher salt

2 cups whole wheat flour, to seal vessel

1 tomato, finely chopped

2 cups spinach, chopped

½ teaspoon cumin powder

1 tablespoon butter

1 bay leaf

½ cup paneer cubes

½ cup cilantro, finely chopped, for garnish

COOKING TIPS

- The longer the meat is marinated, the richer the flavor.
- The process of covering and sealing the lid with the dough is called "*dum* cooking," a slow-cooking process that brings out the flavors of the dish.

Heat 1 tablespoon of the ghee in a pan over medium heat. Add the sliced onion and sauté until golden brown. Next, add the brown cardamom, green cardamom, cloves, ½ teaspoon of the cumin seeds, the cinnamon stick, and the peppercorns—sautéing for about 1 minute until fragrant. Turn off the heat and let it cool completely.

Once cooled, transfer the onion and spice mixture to a blender or food processor. Add 4 cloves of the garlic, half of the chopped ginger, and 2 of the green chiles and blend to create a smooth paste.

In a large mixing bowl, combine the mutton with the prepared onion-spice paste, yogurt, red chili powder, coriander powder, ¼ teaspoon of the turmeric powder, and ¼ teaspoon of the garam masala powder. Add salt to taste. Mix thoroughly, cover the bowl, and marinate in the refrigerator for at least 2 hours, or preferably overnight.

While the mutton marinates, prepare the sealing dough by kneading the whole wheat flour with a little water at a time until a stiff, firm dough is formed.

In a separate sauté pan, heat the remaining 1 tablespoon ghee over medium heat. Add the remaining ginger, 4 cloves garlic, and 2 green chiles and sauté for a few seconds. Stir in the tomato and remaining ¼ teaspoon turmeric powder and sauté until the tomato softens.

Next, add the chopped spinach, cumin powder, and the remaining ¼ teaspoon garam masala powder. Sauté until the spinach wilts, about 5 minutes. Turn off the heat, set aside to cool, and then pulse the mixture in a blender to make a smooth purée.

To cook the mutton, melt the butter in a heavy-bottomed pan or over medium heat. Add the marinated mutton and sauté for about 10 minutes until the oil begins to separate from the sides of the pan. Add 1 cup of water and bring to a boil. Cover the pan with a tight-fitting lid. Use the prepared wheat dough to roll out a rope and firmly seal the lid around the entire rim to create an airtight seal. Turn the heat to low and cook the mutton for about 1 hour.

Turn off the heat and carefully remove and discard the dough seal. To finish the curry, melt the butter in a separate frying pan over medium heat. Add the remaining ½ teaspoon cumin seeds and the bay leaf. Sauté for a few seconds. Stir in the puréed spinach mixture and paneer cubes and bring the gravy to a brisk boil. Add salt to taste. Stir the cooked mutton into the spinach mixture and simmer for 5 minutes to combine the flavors. Transfer the finished curry to a serving dish, garnish generously with cilantro, and serve hot.

Chicken Tikka Masala

CREAMY AND SPICY CHICKEN CURRY

YIELD: 4 SERVINGS

A creamy, spiced tomato curry with charred chicken tikka, this beloved dish is rooted in North Indian and Mughlai cuisine. Its smoky, buttery flavors make it a favorite at family gatherings.

GINGER-GARLIC PASTE

2 inches ginger, peeled and chopped

6 cloves garlic

2 green chiles, chopped

MARINADE

2 teaspoons Kashmiri red chili powder

1 teaspoon lemon juice

½ teaspoon turmeric powder

1 teaspoon garam masala

1 teaspoon black salt (*kala namak*)

1 tablespoon *kasuri methi*

½ cup plain yogurt

Kosher salt

CHICKEN TIKKA

18 ounces chicken boneless thighs, cubed

3 to 4 tablespoons sunflower or canola oil

TIKKA MASALA GRAVY

2 onions, chopped

1-inch piece fresh ginger, peeled and finely chopped

4 cloves garlic

1 green chile, chopped

2 tablespoons ghee

½ teaspoon turmeric powder

1 tablespoon Kashmiri red chili powder

1 teaspoon cardamom powder

2 teaspoons coriander powder

1 teaspoon cumin powder

1 teaspoon garam masala

Kosher salt

4 tomatoes, chopped and puréed

1 tablespoon honey

1 teaspoon *kasuri methi*

¼ cup fresh double cream

To make the ginger-garlic paste: Into a blender, add the ginger, garlic, and green chiles and blend into a smooth paste. Set aside.

To make the marinade: In a large bowl, add all the ingredients for the marinade. Stir in the ginger-garlic paste. Mix well.

To make the chicken tikka: Massage the marinade into the chicken pieces very thoroughly. Let the chicken marinate for 30 minutes to 1 hour at room temperature or refrigerated.

Heat the oil in a nonstick pan over high heat. Place the marinated chicken in the pan and shallow-fry it until the underside of the chicken turns a deep golden color, about 15 minutes. Flip and cook the other side until golden, 5 to 7 minutes.

To make the tikka masala gravy: Add the onions, ginger, garlic, and green chile into a blender and make into a smooth paste. Set aside.

Heat the ghee in a pan over medium heat; add the ginger-garlic paste and sauté for 4 to 5 minutes, until the paste changes color and the raw aroma goes away. Add the turmeric powder, red chili powder, cardamom powder, coriander powder, cumin powder, garam masala powder, and salt, to taste, and sauté for another 2 to 3 minutes, until the mixture forms a blended aromatic masala.

Stir in the tomato purée, honey, *kasuri methi*, and the cooked chicken tikka pieces. Stir well and cook for 4 to 5 minutes. Check the salt and adjust to taste.

Finally, stir in the cream and bring the tikka masala to a brisk boil for 5 minutes, then remove from the heat. Transfer to a serving dish and serve hot.

Bengali Kosha Murgir Mangsho

CHICKEN IN A RICH, SPICY GRAVY

YIELD: 6 SERVINGS

A true gem from Bengali cuisine, Kosha Murgir Mangsho is a slow-cooked chicken dish rich in bold, earthy spices. The deep caramelization of onions, along with the mustard oil and garam masala, give it an unmistakable flavor. This dish is often enjoyed during special occasions, reminding me of Kolkata's vibrant celebrations where slow-cooked curries like this were at the heart of every meal.

GINGER-GARLIC PASTE

2-inch piece ginger, peeled and finely chopped

6 cloves garlic

MARINADE

½ cup plain yogurt

2 teaspoons red chili powder

1 teaspoon garam masala powder

½ teaspoon turmeric powder

1 tablespoon mustard oil

Kosher salt

18 ounces chicken drumsticks

SPICE POWDER

2 green cardamom pods

1 black cardamom

2 cloves

1-inch piece cinnamon stick

4 dried red chiles

1 tablespoon black peppercorns

2 tablespoons mustard oil

5 onions, thinly sliced

2 bay leaves

2 tablespoons mustard oil

1 tablespoon ghee

To make the ginger-garlic paste: Combine the ginger and garlic and blend well, using a blender or a pestle and mortar. Set aside.

To make the marinade: In a large mixing bowl, add the yogurt, red chili powder, garam masala powder, turmeric powder, mustard oil, and salt, to taste.

Using a sharp knife, make 3 or 4 deep slits on each of the chicken drumsticks. Mix thoroughly in the marinade and let marinate for 2 hours.

To make the spice powder: In a small pan, add all the spice ingredients and roast them over medium heat, until the aromas fill the air, about 3 to 4 minutes. Turn off the heat, let cool, and using a blender or a pestle and mortar, blend the spices into a smooth powder. Set aside.

Heat the mustard oil in a heavy-bottomed pan; add the sliced onions and bay leaves and sauté over low heat, until dark golden brown and caramelized, about 15 minutes. Add the ginger-garlic paste and sauté for 1 minute. Stir the spice powder into the onion masala. Add the marinated chicken and the marinade. Add salt to taste.

Turn the heat to low and combine all the ingredients well. Add ¼ cup of water, cover the pan, and simmer for 30 to 40 minutes on low heat, until a thick gravy forms.

Turn off the heat, add 1 tablespoon of ghee, and stir well. Transfer to a serving bowl and serve hot.

Chicken Vindaloo

GOAN-STYLE SPICY AND TANGY CURRY

YIELD: 6 SERVINGS

A fiery vinegar-infused dish from Goa, Chicken Vindaloo is known for its bold flavors and rich spice blend. Originating from Portuguese influences, this curry has the perfect balance of heat, acidity, and a hint of sweetness. Whenever I make this dish, I'm reminded of the beautiful Goan beaches and the bustling food shacks serving spicy, aromatic vindaloos with warm poi bread.

GINGER-GARLIC PASTE

2-inch piece fresh ginger, peeled and finely chopped

6 cloves garlic

2 green chiles, chopped

18 ounces chicken legs

¼ cup white wine vinegar

½ teaspoon turmeric powder

Kosher salt

¾ ounce tamarind

VINDALOO SPICES

4 cloves

3 green cardamom pods

1-inch piece cinnamon stick

1 tablespoon whole black peppercorns

1 tablespoon cumin seeds

1 tablespoon coriander seeds

1 teaspoon *methi* seeds (fenugreek seeds)

2 bay leaf, torn

6 dried red chiles

CURRY

1 tablespoon coconut oil

1 teaspoon mustard seeds

2 onions, finely chopped

2 sprigs curry leaves, roughly torn

2 tomatoes, finely chopped

1 tablespoon jaggery

To make the ginger-garlic paste: Combine the ginger, garlic, and green chiles and blend well, using a blender or a pestle and mortar. Set aside.

Make diagonal cuts on the surface of the chicken legs and smear them with the prepared ginger-garlic paste, vinegar, turmeric powder, and salt, to taste. Cover and marinate for at least 1 hour.

Soak the tamarind in ½ cup of hot water for 15 minutes. Mash the tamarind, add another ½ cup of water, and extract the pulp to produce 1 cup of tamarind water. Set aside.

To roast the vindaloo spices: Preheat a pan over medium heat; add all the spices and roast for 3 to 4 minutes, until their aroma fills the air. Turn off the heat, let cool, and in a mixer grinder jar, blend to make a smooth powder. Set aside.

To make the curry for the vindaloo: Heat 1 tablespoon of coconut oil in a heavy-bottomed saucepan. Add the mustard seeds and cook until they crackle. Add the onions and sauté until soft, 6 to 8 minutes. Stir in the curry leaves and sauté for a few seconds. Stir in the tomatoes and jaggery and cook until the tomatoes become mushy, 8 to 10 minutes.

Add the marinated chicken and marinade, the vindaloo spice powder, tamarind water, and salt, to taste. Mix everything well, turn the heat to low, cover the pan, and simmer for 30 minutes, until the chicken is cooked and the gravy thickens. Check the salt and spices and adjust according to taste. Transfer to a serving bowl and serve hot.

Mangalorean Chicken Ghee Roast

SPICY, GHEE-FLAVORED CHICKEN CURRY

YIELD: 4 SERVINGS

A dish straight from Mangalore's rich culinary heritage, Chicken Ghee Roast is fiery, bold, and indulgent. The slow-roasted, spice-coated chicken is cooked in aromatic ghee, creating a deep, flavorful experience.

MARINADE

½ cup plain yogurt

½ teaspoon turmeric powder

1 tablespoon lemon juice

18 ounces boneless, skinless chicken breast, cubed

GHEE ROAST MASALA

6 dried red chiles

1 teaspoon *methi* seeds (fenugreek seeds)

1 teaspoon cumin seeds

2 teaspoons coriander seeds

3 cloves

1-inch piece cinnamon stick

1 tablespoon whole black peppercorns

4 cloves garlic

1 tablespoon tamarind paste

3 tablespoons ghee

2 sprigs curry leaves, torn

1 teaspoon jaggery

Kosher salt

To make the marinade: In a large mixing bowl, add the yogurt, turmeric, and lemon juice and mix well. Add the chicken to the mixture and marinate for at least 1 hour.

To make the ghee roast masala: Heat a flat skillet over medium heat. Add the red chiles, fenugreek seeds, cumin seeds, coriander seeds, cloves, cinnamon, and peppercorns. Roast until the aroma of the spices wafts through the air. Stir in the garlic and sauté for 1 minute. Take off the heat and let cool.

Once the spices cool, add them to a mixer grinder jar with the garlic, tamarind paste, and 2 to 3 tablespoons of water. Blend into a smooth paste. Set aside.

Heat the ghee in a pan; add the curry leaves and cook until they crackle. Turn the heat to low; add the marinated chicken and sauté until it is cooked, about 15 minutes.

Add the ghee roast masala into the chicken and mix until well combined. Cook the chicken in the pan until the ghee separates out and reaches the surface, about 10 minutes.

Stir in the jaggery and salt, to taste. Mix well and simmer for 2 to 3 minutes. Transfer to a serving bowl and serve hot.

CHAPTER 6

RICES

Paneer Butter Masala Biryani

FRAGRANT BASMATI RICE WITH CREAMY TOMATO PANEER

YIELD: 4 SERVINGS

A delightful fusion of Paneer Butter Masala and Biryani, this dish brings together the richness of a buttery, mildly spiced paneer curry layered with fragrant, aromatic basmati rice. Every spoonful is creamy, flavorful, and indulgent, making it perfect for special occasions. This dish reminds me of family gatherings where biryani was always a centerpiece, and this version with soft, flavorful paneer is an absolute favorite!

3 tablespoons ghee

2-inch piece fresh ginger, peeled and finely chopped

8 cloves garlic, finely chopped

2 onions, thinly sliced

3 brown cardamom (*badi elaichi*)

2 tomatoes, chopped and puréed

½ teaspoon turmeric powder

1 teaspoon Kashmiri red chili powder

1 teaspoon coriander powder

1 teaspoon garam masala powder

1 tablespoon jaggery

Kosher salt

7 ounces paneer, cubed

¼ cup heavy cream

¼ cup mint leaves, coarsely chopped

1½ cups *jeera samba* (or basmati) rice, washed

In a large biryani pot or cooking pan, heat the ghee over medium heat. Add the ginger, garlic, and onions and cook until the onions turn soft and golden brown, 4 to 5 minutes. Stir in the *badi elaichi*, tomato purée, turmeric powder, red chili powder, coriander powder, garam masala powder, jaggery, and salt, to taste. Mix well and bring the tomato gravy to a brisk boil.

When the gravy begins to boil, add the paneer pieces and cream. Mix well, until you are left with a thick semi-coating of masala on the paneer. Stir in the mint leaves and the *jeera* samba (or basmati) rice, and stir well to combine. Add salt, to taste, and 1½ cups of water and bring the mixture to a boil. Turn the heat to low, cover the pan, and cook until all the water is absorbed, about 30 minutes. Turn off the heat and let the biryani rest for 10 to 15 minutes before stirring. Fluff gently with a fork and serve.

One-Pot Spicy-Egg Biryani

PRESSURE-COOKED RICE AND MASALA EGGS IN A FIERY POT

YIELD: 4 SERVINGS

A quick and flavorful Egg Biryani cooked in a pressure cooker, this dish is a lifesaver when you're craving a delicious biryani but don't have hours to spare! The perfectly spiced boiled eggs are infused with aromatic rice, making each bite wholesome and satisfying. I often turn to this recipe for weeknight dinners when I want a fuss-free yet hearty meal.

GINGER-GARLIC PASTE

2-inch piece ginger, peeled and finely chopped

6 cloves garlic, finely chopped

2 tablespoons ghee

2 onions, thinly sliced

2-inch piece cinnamon stick

4 cardamom pods

2 cloves

1 star anise

1 mace (*javitri*)

4 green chiles, finely chopped

1 tomato, finely chopped

½ teaspoon turmeric powder

1 teaspoon coriander powder

2 teaspoons red chili powder

1 teaspoon garam masala powder

6 hard-boiled eggs, peeled

2 cup *jeera* samba rice (or *govind bhog*)

1 pinch of saffron strands

½ cup plain yogurt

Kosher salt

2 bay leaves

¼ cup mint leaves, finely chopped

To make the ginger-garlic paste: Combine the ginger and garlic and blend well, using a blender or a pestle and mortar. Set aside.

Heat the ghee in a pressure-cooker or electric multi-cooker on medium heat. Add the sliced onions and cook until they soften, about 5 to 7 minutes. Add the ginger-garlic paste and the cinnamon, cardamom, cloves, star anise, mace, and green chiles. Sauté until you can smell the delicious aromas.

Add the chopped tomato, turmeric powder, coriander powder, red chili powder, and garam masala powder and mix well. When the masala is mixed well, add the whole boiled eggs.

Next, add the rice, saffron, yogurt, salt, to taste, bay leaves, and mint. Add 3 cups of water and cook for 2 whistles, then turn the heat to low. Simmer for 3 minutes more and turn off the heat. If cooking in a multi-cooker, use the cooking mode for rice. Let the pressure to release naturally.

Gently fluff the biryani with a fork, transfer to a serving bowl, and serve hot.

PAIRING SUGGESTIONS

Serve with Tomato-Onion-Cucumber Raita (page 160).

Hyderabadi Vegetable Dum Biryani

SLOW-COOKED AROMATIC RICE WITH SAFFRON AND SPICED GARDEN VEGGIES

YIELD: 4 SERVINGS

This traditional Hyderabadi Vegetable Dum Biryani layers fragrant rice with spiced vegetables, saffron, and ghee. Slow-cooked using the *dum* method, it's a flavorful, festive dish perfect for celebrations.

DUM DOUGH

1 cup whole wheat flour

RICE

2 cups *jeera samba* (or basmati) rice

Kosher salt

GINGER-GARLIC PASTE

6 cloves garlic

2-inch piece fresh ginger, peeled and finely chopped

2 green chiles

BIRYANI

3 tablespoons sunflower or canola oil

3 onions, thinly sliced

1-inch piece cinnamon stick

3 cloves

2 bay leaves

1 star anise

1 mace

4 cardamom pods

2 tomatoes, finely chopped

½ teaspoon turmeric powder

1 teaspoon red chili powder

1 teaspoon coriander powder

½ teaspoon garam masala powder

½ cup plain yogurt

2 potatoes, peeled and quartered

½ cup green beans, cut into 1-inch pieces

½ cup carrots, peeled and diced

¼ cup mint leaves, freshly chopped

1 teaspoon saffron strands

2 tablespoons ghee

To make the dough for the *dum* cooking: In a large mixing bowl, add the flour and little water at a time until all the flour comes together to form a firm dough. Set aside. The dough will be used to seal the vessel to *dum* cook the biryani.

To make the rice: In a large saucepan, add the *jeera samba* (or basmati) rice, 2 cups of water, and salt, to taste. Bring to a brisk boil for 4 to 5 minutes, then turn off the heat. Drain any excess water and set aside.

To make the ginger-garlic paste: Blend the ginger, garlic, and green chiles in a mixer grinder until they form a coarse paste. Or use a mortar and pestle to grind the paste by hand. Set aside.

To make the biryani: In a large heavy-bottomed pot, add the oil and preheat over medium heat. Add the onions, ginger-garlic paste, cinnamon, cloves, bay leaves, star anise, mace, and cardamom and stir. Reduce the heat to low and sauté the onion mixture until the onions turn brown and caramelize.

Add the tomatoes and sauté until they are mushy, about 5 minutes. Add the turmeric powder, chili powder, coriander powder, and garam masala powder. Stir in the yogurt, potatoes, green beans, and carrots and simmer for 2 minutes more, until the mixture bubbles and produces a rich aroma.

Next, add the mint leaves, half-cooked rice, and saffron. Adjust the salt and spices according to taste. Add 1½ cups of water and cover the pan.

Elongate the dough into a large log and seal the edges of the pan and lid with the dough so the flavors are contained and the steam does not escape. Turn the heat to low and cook the biryani for about 20 minutes. The delicious aromas will emerge after about 10 to 12 minutes of cooking.

After 20 minutes of *dum* cooking, turn off the heat, and let the biryani rest for 15 minutes. Open the pan and stir gently to combine all the masala and vegetables into the rice. Transfer to a serving bowl and serve hot.

Chicken Donne Biryani

BANGALORE MILITARY-HOTEL CLASSIC WITH GREEN HERB MASALA AND TENDER CHICKEN

YIELD: 4 SERVINGS

A specialty from Bangalore's iconic military hotels, Chicken Donne Biryani is a spicy and aromatic biryani served in *donne* (leaf bowls). Unlike Hyderabadi biryanis, this version has a green masala base made with coriander, mint, and green chiles, giving it a unique flavor. I love how quick this biryani is to prepare, yet it packs so much flavor in every bite!

MARINADE

½ cup plain yogurt

½ teaspoon turmeric powder

1 teaspoon lemon juice

Kosher salt

18 ounces boneless chicken

GREEN BIRYANI MASALA

½ cup cilantro

¼ cup mint leaves

4 green chiles

BIRYANI

2 tablespoons ghee

1 bay leaf

1-inch piece cinnamon stick

3 cloves

2 cardamom pods

2 star anise

2-inch piece fresh ginger, peeled and finely chopped

8 cloves garlic, finely chopped

2 onions, thinly sliced

1½ cups jeera samba (or basmati) rice, washed and drained

To make the marinade: in a large mixing bowl, combine the yogurt, turmeric powder, lemon juice, and salt, to taste.

Massage the marinade into the chicken pieces for 5 minutes, then marinate for at least 30 minutes at room temperature.

To make the green biryani masala: In a mixer or blender jar, combine the cilantro, mint leaves, green chiles, and ¼ cup of water; blend to a thick paste. Transfer to a bowl and set aside.

To make the biryani: In a heavy-bottomed pan, heat the ghee over medium heat. Add the bay leaf, cinnamon stick, cloves, cardamom, and star anise and cook until they sizzle. Once the spices are sizzling, add the ginger, garlic, and sliced onions and sauté until the onions turn golden brown, about 5 minutes.

Next, add in the chicken pieces and the marinade. Mix and continue to cook the mixture for 5 to 7 minutes more, stirring continuously.

Finally, add the green biryani masala, rice, and 2½ cups of water to the pan. Mix well and cover the pan. Turn the heat low and cook for 20 to 25 minutes, until the rice is ready.

Let rest for 10 to 15 minutes before fluffing up the rice with a fork. Transfer to a serving plate and serve piping hot.

PAIRING SUGGESTIONS

Serve with Tomato-Onion-Cucumber Raita (page 160).

Jeera Rice

FRAGRANT CUMIN-FLAVORED GHEE RICE

YIELD: 4 SERVINGS

A simple yet flavorful North Indian–style cumin rice, Jeera Rice is a perfect accompaniment to dals and curries. The nutty aroma of cumin tempered in ghee and the fluffy basmati rice make it a staple in Indian homes. This dish brings back childhood memories of Sunday dal-*chawal* meals, where *jeera* rice added an instant touch of comfort.

1 cup *jeera* samba rice (or any short-grain rice), rinsed well

Kosher salt

2 green chiles, slit

2 cardamom pods (optional)

2 cloves (optional)

2 tablespoons ghee

2 teaspoons cumin seeds (*jeera*)

Place the rice in a pressure cooker or electric multi-cooker, add salt, to taste, the green chiles, and 2 cups of water. Add the cardamom and cloves, if using, to give added flavor.

Cover the pressure cooker and cook for 2 whistles on high heat. Turn the heat to low and simmer for 3 to 4 minutes, then turn off the heat. Or, set the rice timer for the electric multi-cooker and pressure-cook until done. Allow the pressure to release naturally. Let the rice rest for 10 minutes before opening the cooker.

Heat the ghee in a small pan over medium heat. Add the cumin seeds and cook until they crackle and you can smell the roasted aromas. Turn off the heat. Pour the roasted cumin into the cooked rice and, using a slotted spoon, stir the rice gently and fluff it up. Transfer to a serving bowl and serve it with your favorite dal or kadhi.

Bengali-Style Basanti Pulao

SWEET AND SAFFRON-INFUSED GOLDEN RICE

YIELD: 4 SERVINGS

A festive Bengali pulao, Basanti Pulao (or Mishti Pulao) is made with *gobindo bhog* rice, saffron, whole spices, and a touch of sugar, giving it a beautiful yellow color and mild sweetness. This dish is a must-have during Durga Puja feasts, and I love how it pairs beautifully with rich Bengali curries like Kosha Mangsho.

3 tablespoons ghee

¼ cup cashews, halved

¼ cup golden raisins

2 bay leaves

2-inch piece cinnamon stick

2 green cardamom pods

2 cloves

1 pinch of saffron strands

1-inch piece fresh ginger, peeled and grated

1 cup *govind bhog* rice (or any short-grain rice), washed

1 teaspoon turmeric powder

1 tablespoon sugar

Heat a pan with 2 tablespoons of ghee over medium heat; add the cashews and roast them until golden-brown and crisp. Add the golden raisins and stir-fry for about 15 seconds. Set aside.

In a pressure cooker or electric multi-cooker; add 1 tablespoon ghee and stir-fry the bay leaves, cinnamon, green cardamom, and cloves for a few seconds, until the spices begin to release their aroma. Add the ginger and sauté for a few seconds more.

Add the rice, turmeric powder, sugar, and 2 cups of water. Pressure-cook for 2 whistles, turn the heat to low, and simmer for 3 minutes, then turn off the heat. If using an electric multi-cooker, cook in the rice mode until done. Let the pressure release naturally.

Stir in the roasted cashews and raisins. Transfer to a serving bowl and serve warm.

Chettinad Vegetable Pulao

SOUTH INDIAN–SPICED VEGETABLE PILAF

YIELD: 4 SERVINGS

A spicy and aromatic rice dish from Tamil Nadu's Chettinad cuisine, this pulao is infused with bold Chettinad spices, coconut, and vegetables. The warmth of cinnamon, star anise, and fennel creates an irresistible depth of flavor. Every bite reminds me of the vibrant spice markets of Chettinad, where this pulao is a household favorite!

SPICE POWDER

2 cloves

1-inch piece cinnamon stick

1 teaspoon whole black peppercorns

1 teaspoon fennel seeds

1 stone flower

1 teaspoon coriander seeds

2 tablespoons ghee

1 onion, finely chopped

4 cloves garlic, finely chopped

1-inch piece fresh ginger, peeled and finely chopped

2 green chiles, finely chopped

1 carrot, peeled and diced

12 green beans, chopped

2 potatoes, peeled and diced

1 bay leaf, torn

½ teaspoon turmeric powder

1 teaspoon red chili powder

1 cup short-grain rice, rinsed

¼ cup mint leaves, finely chopped

To make the spice powder: Heat a small skillet over medium heat. Add the cloves, cinnamon stick, whole black peppercorns, fennel seeds, stone flower, and coriander seeds and roast for 2 to 3 minutes, until the spices release their aromas and turn a toasted color. Let cool, then use a mixer grinder to blend the spices into a fine powder. Set aside.

Heat 2 tablespoons of ghee in a pressure cooker or electric multi-cooker over medium heat. Add the onion, garlic, ginger, and green chiles and sauté until the onions soften. Add the carrot, green beans, potatoes, bay leaf, turmeric powder, red chili powder, and the freshly ground spice powder. Stir well to combine.

Add the washed rice, salt, and 1½ cups of water to the pressure cooker. Cover and pressure-cook for 2 to 3 whistles. Turn the heat to low and simmer for 3 minutes, then turn off the heat. If cooking in an electric multi-cooker, cook in the rice mode until done.

Let the pulao rest for 10 minutes, then stir in the mint leaves, transfer to a serving bowl, and serve warm.

Methi Matar Pulao

FENUGREEK AND GREEN-PEA RICE

YIELD: 4 SERVINGS

A simple yet nutritious one-pot meal, Methi Matar Pulao combines the earthy flavors of fenugreek (*methi*) leaves and the sweetness of green peas in fragrant basmati or *jeera* samba rice. This dish is a staple winter meal in my home, perfect for a comforting lunch with a bowl of raita and a side of pickle.

2 tablespoons ghee, divided

1 teaspoon cumin seeds

1 teaspoon ginger, peeled and finely chopped

4 cloves garlic, finely chopped

2 green chiles, finely chopped

1 cup frozen green peas, thawed and steamed

2 cardamom pods

2 cloves

1-inch piece cinnamon stick

1 bay leaf, torn

7 ounces *methi* leaves (fenugreek leaves), chopped

½ teaspoon turmeric powder

Kosher salt

1 cup short-grain rice (or basmati), washed

1 cup coconut milk

Heat 1 tablespoon of ghee in a pressure cooker or electric multi-cooker on medium heat. Add the cumin seeds, ginger, garlic, and green chiles. Sauté for a few seconds. Stir in the cardamom, cloves, cinnamon, and bay leaf. Sauté for a few seconds. Add the fenugreek leaves and turmeric powder and sauté until the leaves have softened, 3 to 4 minutes.

Stir in the salt, to taste, and the rice. Add the coconut milk and 1 cup of water. Cover the pressure cooker and pressure-cook for 2 to 3 whistles. Turn the heat to low and simmer for 3 minutes. If using an electric multi-cooker, cook using the rice mode. Allow the pressure to release naturally.

Stir in the steamed peas and 1 tablespoon of ghee. Transfer to a serving bowl and serve warm.

Paneer Matar Pulao

COTTAGE CHEESE AND GREEN-PEA RICE

YIELD: 4 SERVINGS

A protein-packed one-pot meal, Paneer Matar Pulao is a flavorful rice dish made with soft paneer cubes, green peas, and aromatic whole spices. It's mild, nutritious, and perfect for a quick lunch or dinner. This dish reminds me of my childhood, when my mother used to make it for lunchboxes—light yet fulfilling!

2 tablespoons ghee

1 cup short-grain rice (or basmati), washed

1-inch piece fresh ginger, peeled and finely chopped

6 cloves garlic, finely chopped

2 onions, thinly sliced

2 green chiles, finely chopped

2 cardamom pods

½-inch cinnamon stick

2 cloves

1 bay leaf

7 ounces paneer, cubed

¼ cup frozen green peas, thawed

Kosher salt

2 sprigs mint leaves, finely chopped

Heat the ghee in a pressure cooker or electric multi-cooker on medium heat. Add the ginger, garlic, onions, and green chiles. Sauté until the onions soften. Stir in the cardamom, cinnamon, cloves, and bay leaf. Sauté for 30 to 40 seconds more.

Stir in the paneer, green peas, rice, and salt, to taste. Add 1½ cups of water. Cover the pressure cooker and pressure-cook for 2 to 3 whistles. Turn the heat to low and simmer for 3 minutes more. If using an electric multi-cooker, cook using the rice mode. Turn off and allow the pressure to release naturally.

Stir in the mint leaves. Transfer to a serving bowl and serve warm.

Thakkali Sadam

SPICY TOMATO RICE FROM TAMIL NADU

YIELD: 4 SERVINGS

A popular South Indian comfort food, Thakkali Sadam is a vibrant, spicy tomato rice cooked with mustard seeds, curry leaves, and dried red chiles. This dish reminds me of quick lunchbox meals and road trips where it was often packed with crispy *papad* and a pickle!

1 cup short-grain rice (or basmati), washed

3 tablespoons ghee

Kosher salt

1 teaspoon cumin seeds

½ teaspoon mustard seeds

1 onion, finely chopped

1-inch piece fresh ginger, peeled and finely chopped

4 cloves garlic, finely chopped

3 tomatoes, finely chopped

1 carrot, peeled and grated

1 sprig curry leaves, finely chopped

2 teaspoons *sambar* powder

½ teaspoon turmeric powder

1 teaspoon cardamom powder

¼ cup mint leaves (*pudina*), finely chopped

In a pressure cooker or electric multi-cooker, add the rice, 1 tablespoon of the ghee, 1½ cups of water, and salt, to taste. Cook for 20 minutes on medium heat. Let cool, then fluff up the rice with a fork and set aside.

Heat 1 tablespoon of ghee in a heavy-bottomed saucepan; add the cumin seeds and mustard seeds; and allow them to crackle for about 15 seconds. Next, add the onion, ginger, and garlic and sauté until the onion is tender and golden. Add the tomatoes and grated carrot; sauté until they are tender and the moisture has evaporated. Continue to cook until the mixture looks like a semi-thick paste, about 10 minutes.

Stir in the chopped curry leaves, *sambar* powder, turmeric powder, cardamom powder, and salt, to taste. Mix well.

Add the mint leaves and sauté for 2 to 3 minutes more.

Gradually stir the cooked rice into the tomato mixture and fold gently so that all the ingredients are well combined. Add the remaining 1 tablespoon of ghee, stir well, and serve hot.

CHAPTER 7

BREADS

Tawa Paratha

CRISP AND FLAKY INDIAN FLATBREAD

YIELD: 8 *TAWA* PARATHAS

A popular North Indian flatbread, Tawa Paratha is slightly crispy, layered, and cooked with ghee or butter, making it flaky and rich. I love the contrast between the crisp outer layer and the soft, buttery inside—it's the perfect accompaniment to rich gravies and dals!

1 cup whole wheat flour, plus more for dusting

½ teaspoon salt

Sunflower or canola oil, for kneading

Ghee, for cooking

In a large bowl, combine the flour, salt, and 1 tablespoon of oil. Knead, adding a little water at a time, until a firm and smooth dough forms.

Add 1 tablespoon of oil to coat the dough and knead again. Cover and set aside for 15 minutes. Knead again, then divide the dough into 8 equal portions.

Roll the dough portions into balls and flatten them with the palm of your hand. Toss in flour and roll them out into circles approximately 3 inches in diameter. Spread ¼ teaspoon oil on each dough circle.

To make a triangle, fold each dough round into a semicircle, then in half again. Toss each triangle in flour, then gently roll each one into a larger triangle.

Heat a cast-iron skillet over medium-high heat.

Place 1 paratha on the skillet for a few seconds until an air pocket pops out. Flip it, then pour ½ teaspoon of ghee on top. Use a spatula to lightly press and turn the paratha. Flip, then press and turn again. Brown spots will appear around the paratha, and it will be slightly crisp.

Continue with the remaining dough and stack the cooked parathas on a platter one on top of the other. Serve with your favorite curry or dal.

Pudina Lachha Paratha

LAYERED MINT PARATHA

YIELD: 8 PARATHAS

A refreshing and aromatic variation of the classic *lachha* paratha, Pudina Lachha Paratha is made by layering fresh mint leaves, whole wheat flour, and ghee, resulting in a crispy and flaky textured bread. This paratha is a personal favorite, as it brings a burst of freshness to any meal!

2 cups whole wheat flour, plus more for dusting

2 green chiles, finely minced

¼ cup mint leaves (*pudina*), finely chopped

Kosher salt

2 tablespoons sunflower or canola oil

Ghee, for cooking and greasing

COOKING TIPS

- If using a cast-iron skillet, grease the skillet well before heating.
- The flour and ghee help the paratha split into the layers you're looking for.

In a large mixing bowl, combine the flour, green chiles, mint leaves, and salt, to taste. Add water a little at a time and knead to make a smooth, firm dough. Drizzle 2 tablespoons of oil on the dough and knead for 5 minutes more. Divide the dough into 8 lemon-size balls.

Heat a skillet over medium heat.

Dust 1 dough ball with flour and roll it into a 6-inch-diameter circle. Smear with ghee or oil and dust with more flour.

Fold the dough like an accordion. Start from one end and work toward the other, making a pleat. Once you have stacked up all the pleats one over the other, roll the dough into a jelly roll. Flatten between the palm of your hands, dust in flour, and roll into a 4- to 5-inch diameter circle. You should see the layers very clearly.

Place the rolled, layered dough on the preheated skillet. Cook on medium heat on both sides for a few seconds each, then smear with ghee and cook until golden brown, crisp, and cooked through completely.

Repeat for the remaining portions of the paratha dough. Place them on a serving platter and serve hot.

PAIRING SUGGESTIONS

Serve with Baingan Bharta (page 64), Creamy Dhaba-Style Dal Makhani (page 78), Spicy Chickpeas Aloo Salad (page 147), and Mooli Raita (page 156).

Methi Thepla

GUJARATI-SPICED FLATBREAD

YIELD: 15 TO 18 *THEPLAS*

A traditional Gujarati staple, Methi Thepla is a lightly spiced, soft flatbread made with fresh fenugreek leaves (*methi*), whole wheat flour, and yogurt, making it nutritious and flavorful. It's one of my go-to travel foods because it stays soft for hours!

2 cups whole wheat flour

½ teaspoon turmeric powder

½ teaspoon red chili powder

¼ teaspoon asafetida

Kosher salt

½ cup *methi* leaves (fenugreek leaves), finely chopped

2 tablespoons plain yogurt

2 tablespoons sunflower or canola oil plus ½ teaspoon

COOKING TIPS

- Stacking prevents the *methi theplas* from drying out, preserving moisture and keeping the texture soft.
- These flatbreads are cooked on high heat and, hence, cook very fast, which can produce smoke. Make sure to have the extractor fan on or the windows open. If you find the high heat inconvenient, reduce it to medium.

In a large bowl, combine the whole wheat flour, turmeric powder, chili powder, asafetida powder, salt, to taste, and fenugreek leaves. Add the yogurt to the flour mixture and knead into a firm, smooth dough, adding a little water at a time. Add 2 tablespoons of oil to coat the dough and knead until it is firm and smooth. Cover and let rest for 15 minutes.

Preheat a cast-iron skillet over high heat.

Divide the *thepla* dough into 15 to 18 equal portions. Roll each portion into a ball and flatten with the palm of your hand. Dust them in flour and roll them out into thin circles about 6 inches in diameter. As you roll, dust them in flour to prevent sticking.

With the skillet on high heat, place the first rolled-out dough on the skillet. After a few seconds, small air pockets will pop out. Flip, then smear about ½ teaspoon of oil on top. Using a flat spatula, press lightly and rotate in the skillet. Flip, then press and turn again. Brown spots will appear around the cooked *thepla*. Remove from heat and place on a flat plate.

Continue for the remaining dough pieces until all are cooked. Stack the *theplas* one on top of the other. Serve hot.

PAIRING SUGGESTIONS

Serve with Aloo Methi Sabzi (page 56), Gujarati Dal (page 79), Classic Sliced Salad (page 142), and Palak Raita (page 157).

Soft Phulkas

FLUFFY INDIAN WHOLE WHEAT FLATBREAD

YIELD: 10 *PHULKAS*

A staple in every Indian household, *phulkas* are soft, puffy, and light whole wheat rotis that pair beautifully with curries, dals, and sabzis. The magic of *phulkas* lies in their simplicity—they are cooked on a direct flame, making them balloon up into soft, airy bread. Every meal in my home feels incomplete without fresh, homemade *phulkas* brushed with a touch of ghee!

1 cup whole wheat flour, plus more for tossing

½ teaspoon kosher salt

1 teaspoon sunflower or canola oil

Ghee, for serving (optional)

COOKING TIPS

- Roll out the batch of dough at once to speed the cooking process.
- Toss the dough in flour as you work to prevent it from getting sticky.

In a large bowl, combine the flour and salt; add ½ to ⅔ cup warm water, a tablespoon at a time, to create a firm dough. Add the oil to coat the dough and knead for 2 to 3 minutes until smooth. Cover and set aside to rest for 15 minutes. Knead again, then divide into 10 equal portions.

Roll the portions of *phulka* dough into balls; flatten them with the palm of your hand. Take 1 portion of dough, toss it in flour, and, using a rolling pin, roll out into a thin circle about 6 inches in diameter. Repeat for the remaining dough balls.

To cook on a gas stove: Preheat a cast-iron skillet over medium-high heat.

Place 1 dough portion on the hot skillet. In a few seconds, small air pockets will form. At this point, flip the rolled dough to the other side.

After a few seconds, turn the flame to high; using tongs, take the dough off the skillet and place it directly on the flame. It should balloon into a spherical shape and puff up.

Remove from the heat, place the *phulka* on a plate and, optionally, spread ghee on 1 side. Continue until all the portions are cooked; stack them one on top of the other and serve hot.

To cook on an electric stove: Preheat a cast-iron skillet over medium-high heat.

Place 1 dough portion on the hot skillet. In a few seconds, small air pockets will form. At this point, flip the rolled dough to the other side.

Flip again and cook the first side, pressing it lightly with a napkin. The dough should puff out. Flip and cook the other side for a few seconds more.

Remove from the heat, place the *phulka* on a plate and, optionally, spread ghee on 1 side. Continue until all the portions are cooked; stack them one on top of the other and serve hot.

PAIRING SUGGESTIONS

Serve with Kerala-Style Avial (page 72), Begun Bhaja (page 61), steamed rice, Hesarukalu Bele Kosambari (page 145), and Beet Raita (page 154).

Puri

DEEP-FRIED INDIAN BREAD

YIELD: 20 PURIS

A festive and celebratory Indian bread, Puri is a crispy, deep-fried whole wheat bread that puffs up beautifully and pairs well with curries and sweets. My fondest memories of puris are from childhood Sunday brunches with a bowl of aloo sabzi and *halwa*!

2 cups whole wheat flour

1 teaspoon kosher salt

3 teaspoons sunflower or canola oil, for kneading, plus 2 to 3 cups, for deep frying

In a large bowl, combine the flour and salt, then add 2 teaspoons of oil. Add a little water at a time to the flour mixture and knead well to make a firm and smooth dough.

Add 1 teaspoon of oil to coat the dough and knead again. Cover and set aside for 15 minutes. Punch down the dough, knead for 1 minute more. Divide the dough into 20 equal portions.

Preheat the oil in a deep-frying pan over medium heat. You will need enough oil to achieve a depth of about 1 to 1½ inches for proper deep-frying.

In the meantime, using a rolling pin, roll out each ball into 5- to 7-inch circles, tossing in a little oil while rolling to prevent the dough from sticking to the work surface. Repeat for the remaining dough. Set aside.

When the oil is 375°F, gently slip one rolled-out piece of dough into the oil. Fry the puri and, using a spatula, continuously yet gently pour oil onto the frying dough and let it puff up.

Once the puri puffs, turn it over and fry for just a few seconds. Using the slotted spatula, drain the oil by the side of the pan and remove from the heat. Place the fried puris on paper towels to absorb excess oil. Continue frying the remaining rolled portions. Serve hot.

PAIRING SUGGESTIONS

Serve with Aloo Methi Sabzi (page 56), Amritsari Chole Masala (page 87), Beet Salad (page 148), Jeera Rice (page 118), and Tomato-Onion-Cucumber Raita (page 160).

Bhatura

SOFT AND FLUFFY DEEP-FRIED BREAD

YIELD: 10 TO 12 BHATURAS

A soft, slightly tangy, deep-fried bread, bhatura is an iconic Punjabi dish often served with *chole* (chickpea curry). The airy, chewy texture of fermented dough fried until golden makes it an indulgent treat. The first time I made bhaturas at home, the way they puffed up in the oil was pure joy!

2 cups all-purpose flour (*maida*)

1 tablespoon fine semolina (*sooji/rava*)

1 teaspoon *kalonji* (nigella seeds)

1½ teaspoons active dry yeast

1 tablespoon sugar

1½ teaspoons kosher salt

¼ cup plain yogurt

2 tablespoons sunflower or canola oil, for kneading, plus 2 to 3 cups, for deep frying

In a large mixing bowl, add the flour, semolina, *kalonji,* yeast, sugar, and salt. Make a well in the center of the flour mixture and add the yogurt and 3 tablespoons of lukewarm water, 1 or 2 teaspoons at a time. Knead to make a smooth dough.

Oil the palms of your hands with 1 tablespoon of oil. Pour the remaining 1 tablespoon of oil over the dough and knead until it becomes smooth and shiny, about 10 minutes. As you work, add more flour if the dough is too sticky. Cover the bowl with a dish towel and let the dough rest for at least 1 hour, until it has risen and doubled in size.

Punch down the dough, knead gently, and divide it into 10 to 12 equal portions. Using a rolling pin, quickly roll out each dough portion into a 5-inch-diameter circle.

Preheat the oil in a deep-frying pan over medium heat. You will need enough oil to achieve a depth of about 1 to 1½ inches for proper deep-frying.

When the oil reaches 375°F, gently slip 1 piece of rolled-out dough into the oil. Fry, turning once until it is puffed up, cooked, and lightly browned, about 40 to 50 seconds.

Using a slotted spoon, lift the bhatura from the oil and place it on paper towels to drain. It should be light and spongy. Fry the remaining portions one at a time. Serve warm.

PAIRING SUGGESTIONS

Serve with Amritsari Chole Masala (page 87), Palak Paneer (page 95), Chatpata Rajma Salad (page 140), Jeera Rice (page 118), and Palak Raita (page 157).

CHAPTER 8

SALADS

Chatpata Rajma Salad

ZINGY KIDNEY-BEAN SALAD WITH CHAAT MASALA AND FRESH HERBS

YIELD: 4 TO 6 SERVINGS

A protein-packed salad, Chatpata Rajma Salad combines boiled kidney beans, crunchy veggies, chaat masala, and lemon juice, creating a tangy, spicy, and wholesome dish. This salad is perfect as a light meal or as a side with parathas. I love making this when I want something nutritious yet super flavorful!

2 cups *rajma* (red kidney beans), soaked overnight

Kosher salt

1 onion, finely chopped

1 tomato, finely chopped

2 green chiles, finely chopped

1 teaspoon chaat masala powder

1 lemon, juiced

¼ cup mint leaves (*pudina*), finely chopped

COOKING TIP

- You can use canned kidney beans for this recipe. Drain and wash the beans before making the salad.

Add the kidney beans, salt, to taste, and 5 to 6 cups of water to a pressure cooker. Cook on medium heat for 40 minutes. If using an electric multi-cooker, cook for 30 minutes. Let the pressure release naturally. The *rajma* should be soft. Drain any excess water and let the *rajma* cool completely.

Into a mixing bowl, add the cooked *rajma*, onion, tomato, green chiles, chaat masala powder, lemon juice, mint leaves, and salt, to taste. Mix well to combine. Serve chilled.

PAIRING SUGGESTIONS

Serve with Paneer Butter Masala Biryani (page 112), Dal Tadka (page 76), Pudina Lachha Paratha (page 131), and Mooli Raita (page 156).

Classic Sliced Salad

CRUNCHY CUCUMBER, TOMATO, AND ONION MEDLEY WITH LEMON AND SALT

YIELD: 4 TO 6 SERVINGS

A staple in every Indian *thali*, this Classic Sliced Salad is a simple yet refreshing combination of cucumbers, tomatoes, onions, carrots, and radishes arranged beautifully on a plate. The crunch and natural sweetness of the vegetables pair well with all Indian meals. This salad always reminds me of the vibrant *thali* spreads served in *dhabas*!

- 1 carrot, thinly sliced
- 1 cucumber, peeled and sliced
- 1 tomato, sliced
- 1 onion, sliced
- Kosher salt
- ½ teaspoon freshly ground black pepper
- 1 lemon, halved

On a serving plate, arrange the carrots at the edge of the plate. Next, arrange the sliced cucumbers, followed by the tomato slices, then the onion slices.

Sprinkle with salt, to taste, and grind pepper over the top of the salad. Squeeze the lemon halves over the top and serve.

PAIRING SUGGESTIONS

Serve with any meal or pair it along with Baingan Bharta (page 64), Dhaba-Style Dal Palak (page 89), Tawa Paratha (page 128), Tomato-Onion-Cucumber Raita (page 160), and Green Chutney (page 164).

Raw Mango-Cucumber Salad with Roasted Peanuts

TANGY GREEN MANGO, COOL CUCUMBER, AND NUTTY PEANUT CRUNCH

YIELD: 4 TO 6 SERVINGS

A refreshing summer salad, Raw Mango-Cucumber Salad is a tangy mix of raw mango, cucumbers, peanuts, and spices, bringing together sweet, sour, and nutty flavors. It's a favorite during the mango season, and I always make it as a cooling side for spicy Indian meals!

1 raw mango, peeled and chopped
1 cucumber, peeled and chopped
¼ cup roasted peanuts
1 tablespoon honey
2 green chiles, finely chopped
½ teaspoon chili powder
¼ cup mint leaves, chopped
Kosher salt

In a large mixing bowl, add the mango, cucumber, peanuts, honey, green chiles, chili powder, and mint leaves. Add salt, to taste.

Toss well and transfer to a serving bowl and serve cold as a side dish.

PAIRING SUGGESTIONS

Serve with any meal or pair with Baingan Bharta (page 64), Gujarati Dal (page 79), Soft Phulkas (page 134), and Green Chutney (page 164).

Hesarukalu Bele Kosambari

KARNATAKA-STYLE MOONG DAL AND CUCUMBER SALAD WITH COCONUT

YIELD: 4 TO 6 SERVINGS

A traditional Karnataka-style salad, Hesarukalu Bele Kosambari is a light, protein-rich dish made with soaked *moong* dal, fresh cucumber, and coconut. It's commonly served during festivals and *pujas*, and I love its mild yet satisfying taste.

1 cup whole green *moong* dal, sprouted

1 carrot, peeled and grated

½ cup fresh coconut, grated

1 cucumber, finely chopped

1 tomato, finely chopped

2 green chiles, finely chopped

1 lemon, juiced

6 sprigs cilantro, finely chopped

Kosher salt

SEASONING

1 teaspoon coconut oil

½ teaspoon mustard seeds

1 teaspoon white urad dal (split)

1 sprig curry leaves, finely chopped

SERVING TIP

- The salad can be served at room temperature or chilled.

In a large mixing bowl, combine the sprouts, carrot, coconut, cucumber, tomato, green chiles, lemon, cilantro, and salt, to taste. Mix well.

To make the seasoning: Heat the oil in a small pan; add the mustard seeds and urad dal and cook until the seeds crackle and the dal turns golden brown and crisp. Turn off the heat and stir in the curry leaves.

Add the seasoning to the *moong* sprout salad and stir well to combine. Check the taste and adjust salt accordingly. Transfer to a serving bowl and serve.

PAIRING SUGGESTIONS

Serve with any meal or pair with Kerala-Style Avial (page 72), Arachuvitta Sambar (page 84), steamed rice, and Beet Raita (page 154).

Carrot, Tomato, and Cucumber Salad

LIGHTLY GRATED TRI-VEGGIE SLAW WITH A HINT OF CITRUS

YIELD: 4 TO 6 SERVINGS

This quick and nutritious grated salad is made with carrots, tomatoes, and cucumbers, offering a light, refreshing, and mildly sweet flavor. I love making this salad as a quick side dish with roti and dal—it adds the perfect freshness to a meal!

2 cups carrots, peeled and grated

1 cucumber, peeled and finely chopped

2 tomatoes, finely chopped

2 green chiles, finely chopped

¼ cup cilantro, finely chopped

½ teaspoon sugar

1 lemon, juiced

Kosher salt

In a large mixing bowl, add the carrots, cucumber, tomatoes, green chiles, cilantro, sugar, lemon juice, and salt, to taste.

Toss well and check for seasonings and adjust, if required. Transfer to a serving bowl and serve as a side dish.

Spicy Chickpeas Aloo Salad

STREET-STYLE TANGY CHAAT

YIELD: 4 TO 6 SERVINGS

A spicy and tangy street-style *chaat* salad, this dish combines boiled chickpeas, potatoes, *chaat* masala, and a drizzle of tamarind chutney. Every bite is packed with crunch, spice, and tang, making it an irresistible snack or side dish. It's commonly served during festivals and *pujas*, and I love its mild yet satisfying taste.

1 cup *kabuli* chana (white chickpeas), soaked overnight

Kosher salt

1 onion, finely chopped

1 potato, boiled, peeled, and diced

1 tomato, finely chopped

1 green chile, finely chopped

½ teaspoon black salt (*kala namak*)

¼ teaspoon black pepper powder

½ teaspoon *chaat* masala powder

1 lemon, juiced

¼ cup cilantro, finely chopped, for garnish

COOKING TIP

- You can use canned chickpeas for this recipe. Drain and wash them before making the salad.

To a pressure cooker, add the chickpeas, kosher salt, to taste, and enough water to cover them. Cook for about 40 minutes. If using an electric multi-cooker, cook for 30 minutes. Let the pressure release naturally. The chickpeas should be soft in texture. Drain any excess water and set the *rajma* aside. Let cool completely.

In a mixing bowl, combine the chickpeas, onion, potato, tomato, green chile, black salt, pepper powder, *chaat* masala, lemon juice, and kosher salt, to taste. Garnish with cilantro and serve immediately or chill and serve later.

Beet Salad

SIMPLY STEAMED BEETS WITH LEMON, PEPPER, AND CORIANDER

YIELD: 4 TO 6 SERVINGS

A simple yet vibrant salad, this steamed Beet Salad is naturally sweet, packed with nutrients and lightly seasoned with salt, lemon juice, *chaat* masala powder, and a hint of pepper. Steaming the beets enhances their natural sweetness, making this a perfect side dish for any Indian meal. This reminds me of my grandmother's traditional *thali*, where a small bowl of beet salad was always served with dal and rice.

4 beets

Kosher salt

Freshly ground black pepper

Cumin powder, for sprinkling

Chaat masala powder, for sprinkling

1 lemon, juiced

Wash, peel, and halve the beets. Place them in a pressure cooker or electric multi-cooker with a ½ cup of water.

Pressure-cook for 6 to 7 whistles or if using an electric multi-cooker, cook for 5 minutes. Turn off the heat and let the pressure release naturally. Let the beets cool to room temperature.

Thinly slice and arrange the beets on a platter. Sprinkle with salt, to taste, the pepper, cumin powder, *chaat* masala powder, and lemon juice. Serve chilled.

PAIRING SUGGESTIONS

Serve with any meal or pair with Aloo Methi Sabzi (page 56), Dal Tadka (page 76), Tawa Paratha (page 128), and Green Chutney (page 164).

Khamang Kakdi

MAHARASHTRA-STYLE CUCUMBER AND PEANUT SALAD

YIELD: 4 TO 6 SERVINGS

A traditional Maharashtrian salad, Khamang Kakdi is a refreshing, crunchy cucumber salad tossed with roasted peanuts, fresh coconut, and a mustard seed tempering. The combination of crunchy peanuts, cooling cucumber, and fragrant tempering makes this salad light yet satisfying. Every bite reminds me of traditional Maharashtrian meals where this salad adds a delicious crunch!

2 cucumbers, peeled and chopped

½ cup fresh coconut, grated

3 tablespoons roasted peanuts, coarsely pounded

2 tablespoons plain yogurt

¼ cup cilantro, finely chopped

Kosher salt

SEASONING

½ teaspoon sunflower or canola oil

1 teaspoon mustard seeds

¼ teaspoon asafetida

2 green chiles, finely chopped

1 sprig curry leaves, coarsely chopped

In a large mixing bowl, add the cucumbers, coconut, peanuts, yogurt, cilantro, and salt, to taste. Mix well.

To make the seasoning: Heat the oil in a pan over medium heat. Add the mustard seeds and asafetida. Let the mixture crackle for about 10 seconds, then add the green chiles and curry leaves and sauté for another 15 seconds. Add the seasoning to the salad and mix well.

Transfer to a serving bowl and serve immediately or chill in the fridge to serve later.

CHAPTER 9

RAITAS

Beet Raita

VIBRANT PINK YOGURT DIP WITH SWEET GRATED BEETROOT

YIELD: 4 TO 6 SERVINGS

This beautifully pink, mildly sweet, and earthy raita is made with grated beets, yogurt, and a touch of cumin and black salt. It is cooling, nutrient-dense, and visually stunning, making it a perfect side for both everyday meals and festive occasions. I love serving this raita with parathas or spicy biryanis!

2 cups plain yogurt

1 teaspoon cumin powder

Black salt (*kala namak*)

½ teaspoon sunflower or canola oil

1 beet, peeled and finely grated

SEASONING

½ teaspoon sunflower or canola oil

½ teaspoon mustard seeds

½ teaspoon white urad dal (split)

2 green chiles, finely chopped

1 sprig curry leaves, finely chopped

In a mixing bowl, add the yogurt, cumin powder, and salt, to taste, and whisk until smooth.

Heat the oil in a pan over medium heat, add the grated beet and a pinch of salt, and sauté until the beet is slightly softened. Remove from the heat and let cool.

Stir the cooled beet into the yogurt mixture and combine well. Transfer to a serving bowl.

To make the seasoning: Heat the oil in a small pan over medium heat. Add the mustard seeds and urad dal and let the seeds crackle and the dal turn golden brown. Stir in the green chiles and curry leaves. Let cool.

Pour the seasoning over the beet raita and serve chilled.

PAIRING SUGGESTIONS

Serve with any meal or pair with Aloo Methi Sabzi (page 56), Dhaba-Style Dal Palak (page 89), and Tawa Paratha (page 128).

Mooli Raita

ZESTY RADISH YOGURT RELISH WITH CUMIN AND SALT

YIELD: 4 SERVINGS

A spicy and earthy raita, Mooli Raita is made with grated radishes, yogurt, and simple spices, creating a bold and refreshing side dish. The strong flavor of radish blends beautifully with the coolness of yogurt, making this raita an excellent companion for heavy meals.

2 cups plain yogurt

¼ teaspoon red chili powder

1 teaspoon cumin powder

Kosher salt

2 radishes (*mooli*), grated

1 green chile, finely chopped

6 sprigs cilantro, finely chopped (or dill leaves)

In a bowl, whisk the yogurt, red chili powder, cumin powder, and salt, to taste, until well combined.

Add the grated *mooli*, green chile, and cilantro to the yogurt and mix well. Check the salt and spices and adjust to suit your taste. Serve chilled.

PAIRING SUGGESTIONS

Serve with any meal or pair with Baingan Bharta (page 64), Dal Tadka (page 76), Pudina Lachha Paratha (page 131), and Green Chutney (page 164).

Palak Raita

SILKY, LIGHTLY SPICED SPINACH-INFUSED YOGURT

YIELD: 4 SERVINGS

A nutritious and refreshing raita, Palak Raita is made with blanched spinach, creamy yogurt, and mild spices, making it a perfect cooling side dish for spicy Indian meals. The vibrant green color and earthy flavor of spinach blend beautifully with the tanginess of yogurt. I love how this raita adds a touch of nutrition to any meal while still keeping it light and delicious!

2 cups plain yogurt

½ teaspoon cumin powder

¼ teaspoon red chili powder

Kosher salt

Sunflower or canola oil

2 cups spinach leaves (*palak*), finely chopped

SEASONING

½ teaspoon sunflower or canola oil

¼ teaspoon mustard seeds

½ teaspoon white urad dal (split)

1 sprig curry leaves, finely chopped

In a mixing bowl, add the yogurt, cumin powder, red chili powder, and salt, to taste. Whisk until smooth.

Heat the oil in a pan; add the chopped spinach, sprinkle with salt, to taste, and sauté until the spinach is wilted. Turn off the heat and let cool.

Add the spinach to the yogurt mixture and stir well to combine. Transfer to a serving bowl.

To make the seasoning: Heat the oil in a small pan over medium heat. Add the mustard seeds and urad dal and cook until the seeds crackle and the dal turns golden brown. Add the curry leaves and stir for a few seconds.

Pour the seasoning over the prepared spinach raita and serve chilled.

Kela Anar Raita

SWEET BANANA AND POMEGRANATE YOGURT RAITA

YIELD: 4 SERVINGS

A sweet and fruity raita, Kela Anar Raita combines ripe banana slices, juicy pomegranate pearls, and thick yogurt, creating a creamy, mildly sweet, and refreshing side dish. It's a great festive raita that pairs well with rich meals or can even be enjoyed as a light dessert. The first time I made this, I was surprised at how well the sweetness of the bananas complemented the tanginess of the yogurt!

2 cups plain yogurt

Kosher salt

¼ teaspoon red chili powder

1 tablespoon Dijon mustard

½ teaspoon cumin powder

1 ripe banana, diced

¼ cup pomegranate seeds

In a large mixing bowl, whisk the yogurt, salt, to taste, red chili powder, Dijon mustard, and cumin powder until smooth and creamy. Stir in the diced banana and pomegranate seeds.

Transfer to a serving dish and refrigerate for 2 hours before serving.

Tomato-Onion-Cucumber Raita

COOLING YOGURT SALAD WITH JUICY TOMATOES, CRUNCHY CUCUMBERS, AND SWEET ONIONS

YIELD: 4 TO 6 SERVINGS

A refreshing and cooling raita, this Tomato-Onion-Cucumber Raita is made with fresh yogurt, finely chopped tomatoes, onions, cucumbers, and mild spices. It is the perfect accompaniment to spicy Indian meals, balancing out heat with its creamy and tangy flavors. I love serving this raita with *pulao* or parathas, especially during summer meals!

2 cups plain yogurt

Kosher salt

½ teaspoon cumin powder

1 cucumber, peeled and finely chopped

1 tomato, finely chopped

1 onion, finely chopped

2 green chiles, finely chopped

In a large mixing bowl, add the yogurt, salt, to taste, and cumin powder and whisk well to combine.

Add the cucumber, tomato, onion, and green chiles and stir well. Check the salt and adjust to suit your taste. Transfer to a serving bowl and serve chilled.

Coorg Mange Pajji

COORG-STYLE SPICED MANGO YOGURT CHUTNEY WITH COCONUT AND GREEN CHILES

YIELD: 4 TO 6 SERVINGS

A traditional yogurt-based dish from Coorg, Mange Pajji is a sweet, tangy, and mildly spicy mango raita with coconut and green chiles. The first time I tasted this raita in Coorg, I was amazed at how well it paired with simple rice dishes. It's the perfect blend of sweet mangoes, creamy yogurt, and aromatic spices!

2 cups plain yogurt

1 teaspoon sugar

Kosher salt

4 tablespoons grated fresh coconut

2 teaspoon mustard seeds

1 green chile, finely chopped

1 mango (ripe), peeled and thinly sliced

SEASONING

1 teaspoon sunflower or canola oil

½ teaspoon mustard seeds

1 dry red chile

1 sprig curry leaves, finely chopped

3 cloves garlic, coarsely chopped

In a large mixing bowl, add the yogurt, sugar, and salt, to taste. Whisk until smooth.

In a separate bowl, make a smooth paste of the coconut, mustard seeds, green chile, and 4 tablespoons of water. Add the paste to the yogurt mixture, then fold in the mango slices. Season with salt, to taste, and mix well. Transfer to a serving bowl.

To make the seasoning: Heat the oil in a small pan over medium heat. Add the mustard seeds, red chile, curry leaves, and garlic and sauté until the garlic browns slightly.

Pour the seasoning over the Coorg Mange Pajji and serve chilled.

CHAPTER 10

CHUTNEYS

Green Chutney

ZESTY CORIANDER-MINT DIP WITH A CITRUS KICK

YIELD: 10 SERVINGS

A classic Indian condiment, Green Chutney is a flavorful and refreshing blend of cilantro, mint, green chiles, and lemon juice. It's a must-have in Indian households, served with snacks, *chaats*, and sandwiches. I love how this chutney instantly brightens up any meal with its zesty and herbaceous flavor!

1 cup cilantro, chopped

1 cup mint leaves, chopped

¼ cup curry leaves

¼ cup roasted peanuts

1-inch piece fresh ginger, peeled and finely chopped

2 green chiles, coarsely chopped

1 tablespoon sugar

1 lemon, juiced

Kosher salt

TIPS

- For a flavor twist, substitute roasted almonds for the roasted peanuts.
- The lemon juice enhances the flavors of the mint and coriander and prevents discoloration of the greens.
- The chutney can be stored in a glass container in the refrigerator for up to 1 week.

Combine the cilantro, mint leaves, curry leaves, peanuts, ginger, green chiles, sugar, lemon juice, and salt, to taste, and grind to a smooth paste in a blender. Add ¼ cup water to blend the chutney well.

Transfer to a glass bowl and serve.

PAIRING SUGGESTIONS

Serve with any meal or appetizer and even add as a topping over chaats.

Tamarind Chutney

SWEET-TANGY DATE AND TAMARIND SAUCE

YIELD: 10 SERVINGS

A must-have for *chaats*, Tamarind Chutney is a sweet, tangy, and slightly spicy sauce made from tamarind pulp, dates, jaggery, and spices. It's a staple in my kitchen, especially when making chaat, samosas, and *pakoras*.

1 cup dates, pitted

½ cup jaggery

¼ cup tamarind, seeded

1 teaspoon red chili powder

1 teaspoon cumin powder

1 teaspoon dry ginger powder

1 teaspoon black salt (*kala namak*)

Kosher salt

STORAGE TIP

- Can be stored for up to 2 weeks in an airtight glass container in the fridge.

In a pressure cooker, add the dates, jaggery, tamarind, and 1 cup of water. Pressure-cook for 3 to 4 whistles. Turn off the heat and let the pressure release naturally. If using an electric multi-cooker, set the timer for 15 minutes.

Using a handheld blender, blend the date mixture to a coarse consistency. Alternatively, put in a blender jar and blend.

Place the puréed chutney back on heat in a saucepan and add the chili powder, cumin powder, dry ginger powder, black salt, and kosher salt, to taste. Add ½ cup of water to adjust the consistency, then simmer for 3 to 4 minutes. Turn off the heat and let cool.

Refrigerate and store in an airtight glass container until ready to serve.

PAIRING SUGGESTIONS

Serve with any meal or appetizer or even add it as a topping over chaats.

Tamil Nadu–Style Coconut Chutney

FRESH COCONUT RELISH WITH CURRY LEAVES AND MUSTARD SEEDS

YIELD: 10 SERVINGS

A staple chutney from Tamil Nadu, Coconut Chutney is a creamy, mildly spiced chutney made with fresh coconut, green chiles, and tempered mustard seeds. It pairs beautifully with *idlis*, *dosas*, and vadas and brings back memories of hearty South Indian breakfasts!

1½ cups fresh coconut, grated

2 green chiles, chopped

1-inch piece fresh ginger, peeled and chopped

Kosher salt

1 lemon, juiced

SEASONING

1 teaspoon sunflower or canola oil

½ teaspoon mustard seeds

1 teaspoon white urad dal (split)

1 sprig curry leaves, finely chopped

1 dry red chile, broken

COOKING TIPS

- If fresh coconut isn't available, use frozen; thaw before use.
- Adding warm or hot water prevents the coconut chutney from curdling and becoming sticky.

In a mixer grinder, add the coconut, green chiles, ginger, salt, to taste, and ¾ cup of lukewarm water; blend to make a smooth coconut chutney. Transfer to a bowl and stir in the lemon juice.

To make the seasoning: Heat the oil in a small pan over medium heat; add the mustard seeds and urad dal and cook until the seeds crackle and the dal turns golden brown. Add the curry leaves and red chiles and stir for a few seconds. Turn off the heat.

Spoon the seasoning over the chutney and serve.

PAIRING SUGGESTIONS

Serve with any breakfast meal or appetizer.

Andhra-Style Peanut Chutney

CREAMY ROASTED PEANUT CHUTNEY WITH TAMARIND AND CHILES

YIELD: 10 SERVINGS

A bold and nutty Andhra-style chutney, this chutney is made with roasted peanuts, red chiles, garlic, and tamarind, creating a spicy, tangy, and creamy chutney that pairs perfectly with *idlis*, *dosas*, and even rotis!

2 teaspoons white urad dal (split)
2 tablespoons chana dal
1 sprig curry leaves, chopped
1 green chile
1 cup roasted peanuts
1-inch piece fresh ginger, peeled and finely chopped
Kosher salt

SEASONING

1 teaspoon ghee
½ teaspoon mustard seeds
¼ teaspoon white urad dal (split)
1 sprig curry leaves
2 dry red chiles

In a pan over medium heat, add the urad dal and chana dal and roast until the dals start to turn light brown and smell toasted and nutty. Add the curry leaves and green chile. Stir for 1 minute, then turn off the heat. Let cool for 5 minutes.

In a blender jar, add the roasted dal mixture, peanuts, ginger, salt, to taste, and ½ cup water and blend to make a smooth paste. Transfer to a bowl and set aside.

To make the seasoning: Heat the ghee in a small pan over medium heat. Add the mustard seeds and urad dal and cook until the seeds crackle and the dal turns golden brown and crisp. Add the curry leaves and red chiles and allow them to splutter as well. Turn off the heat.

Pour the seasoning over the peanut chutney, mix well, and serve.

PAIRING SUGGESTIONS

You can serve the chutney along with any breakfast meal or along with an appetizer.

Roasted Red Bell Pepper Chutney

SMOKY BELL PEPPER PURÉE WITH GARLIC AND TAMARIND

YIELD: 10 SERVINGS

This Roasted Red Bel Pepper Chutney is a smoky, mildly sweet, and tangy chutney made with charred red bell peppers, garlic, red chiles, and tamarind. The roasting process enhances the natural sweetness of the peppers, creating a deep and bold flavor. I love how this chutney adds a vibrant pop of color and a rich depth of taste to any meal!

2 tablespoons sunflower or canola oil, divided

4 red bell peppers, seeded and coarsely chopped

4 dry red chiles

½ cup pearl onions, quartered

4 cloves garlic, chopped

1 tomato, coarsely chopped

Kosher salt

SEASONING

½ teaspoon mustard seeds

1 teaspoon white urad dal (split)

1 sprig curry leaves

2 dry red chiles, crushed

COOKING TIP

- Cover the pan when cooking the bell peppers so they sweat a little and cook faster.

Heat 1 tablespoon of oil over medium heat in a sauté pan; add the bell peppers, red chiles, onions, and garlic and sauté until the onions are transparent and the bell peppers have softened, about 10 minutes. Add the tomato and continue to sauté until the tomato has softened. Add salt, to taste. Turn off the heat and let cool.

Add the chutney mixture to a mixer grinder and blend to make a smooth paste. Check the salt and adjust, to taste. Transfer the chutney to a bowl and set aside.

To make the seasoning: Heat 1 tablespoon of oil in a pan over medium heat, add the mustard seeds and urad dal and cook until the seeds crackle and the dal turns golden brown. Add the red chiles and curry leaves. Stir for 2 to 3 seconds, then turn off the heat.

Add the seasoning to the chutney and serve.

PAIRING SUGGESTIONS

Serve with any breakfast meal or appetizer.

Tomato Chutney

SPICY, TANGY ROASTED-TOMATO SPREAD WITH GARLIC AND RED CHILES

YIELD: 10 SERVINGS

This South Indian–style Tomato Chutney is a bold and tangy condiment made with ripe tomatoes, garlic, red chiles, and a tempered spice mix. It's my favorite chutney to serve with *dosas*, *idlis*, and even parathas for an extra kick of flavor!

2 tablespoons sesame oil, divided

½ cup pearl onions, coarsely chopped

4 tomatoes, coarsely chopped

1 green chile, chopped

¼ teaspoon turmeric powder

Kosher salt

SEASONING

½ teaspoon mustard seeds

1 teaspoon white urad dal (split)

2 dry red chiles

4 curry leaves

Heat 1 tablespoon of sesame oil in a small pan; add the onions and sauté until soft and tender. Add the chopped tomatoes, green chile, turmeric powder, and salt, to taste. Sauté until the tomatoes are nice and soft and almost all the water has evaporated, about 15 minutes. Let the chutney mixture cool, add to a mixer grinder jar or blend, then grind into a smooth paste.

To make the seasoning: Heat 1 tablespoon of sesame oil in another small pan; add the mustard seeds, urad dal, red chiles, and curry leaves and cook until the seeds crackle and the dal turns golden brown.

Pour the seasoning over the ground chutney and stir well. Check the salt and spices and adjust to taste and serve.

PAIRING SUGGESTIONS

Serve with any breakfast meal or appetizer.

CHAPTER 11

DESSERTS

Moong Dal Halwa

LUXURIOUS ROASTED-LENTIL FUDGE WITH SAFFRON AND NUTS

YIELD: 6 TO 8 SERVINGS

A royal and festive Indian dessert, Moong Dal Halwa is a rich, nutty pudding made from yellow *moong* dal, ghee, milk, and sugar. It's a staple at North Indian weddings, where the aroma of roasting *moong* dal in ghee fills the air. This dessert is labor-intensive but worth every bite!

1 cup yellow *moong* dal (split), soaked for 3 hours and drained

1 cup ghee

1 cup sugar

1 cup whole milk

2 pinches saffron strands

COOKING TIPS

- Do not overgrind the dal. You want a coarse mixture, not a paste.
- Resist the urge to turn up the heat when cooking the dal mixture. Cooking over low heat is necessary to achieve the delicious taste, flavor, and aroma you want.

In the jar of a food processor, add the *moong* dal; grind into a coarse mixture.

Heat the ghee in a heavy-bottomed pan over medium heat; add the ground *moong* dal and reduce the heat to low, stirring continuously, until the mixture turns a golden-brown color, at least 45 minutes to 1 hour.

Once the *moong* dal is well roasted, add the sugar, milk, and saffron and mix until well combined. Continue stirring on low heat until the mixture thickens and releases itself from the sides of the pan, 20 to 30 minutes.

Transfer to a serving bowl and serve hot.

Paruppu Payasam

SOUTH INDIAN JAGGERY AND LENTIL PUDDING WITH COCONUT MILK

YIELD: 6 TO 8 SERVINGS

A South Indian festive dessert, Paruppu Payasam is made with yellow lentils, jaggery, coconut milk, and cardamom, creating a sweet, velvety pudding. It's a must-have during Onam and Tamil New Year's feasts, and I love how the jaggery and coconut milk give it a naturally rich and deep flavor!

¼ cup yellow *moong* dal (split)

2 tablespoons chana dal (Bengal gram dal)

1½ cups milk

1 cup coconut milk

2 tablespoons fresh coconut, grated

½ cup jaggery

1 teaspoon cardamom powder (*elaichi*)

ROASTED NUTS

1 tablespoon ghee

10 cashews, halved

Soak the dals in water for 30 minutes.

In a pressure cooker or electric multi-cooker, combine the *moong* dal and chana dal with 1 cup of water and pressure-cook for 4 whistles, or 10 minutes in an electric multi-cooker. Turn off the heat and let the pressure release naturally. Mash the dals just enough to retain a grainy texture. Set aside.

Transfer to a heavy-bottomed pan, add the milk, coconut milk, coconut, jaggery, and cardamom powder. Stir and simmer the dal mixture until the jaggery dissolves, then bring to a brisk boil. Turn the heat to low and simmer until the *payasam* reaches a creamy and pudding-like consistency, 2 to 3 minutes. Transfer to a serving bowl.

To make the roasted nuts: Heat the ghee in a small pan over medium heat; add the cashews and roast them until the nuts turn golden brown. Stir in the nuts. Serve warm or chilled.

Gulab Phirni

SILKY ROSE-INFUSED GROUND-RICE CUSTARD

YIELD: 6 TO 8 SERVINGS

A royal North Indian dessert, Gulab Phirni is a thick and creamy rice pudding flavored with rose water and saffron, traditionally served in earthenware bowls. This dish reminds me of weddings and grand celebrations, where the subtle floral aroma of rose-infused *phirni* makes every bite feel indulgent!

DATES

1 cup pitted dates, finely chopped

½ cup hot whole milk

RICE

¼ cup short-grain rice (or basmati), soaked for 30 minutes and drained

3 cups plus 2 tablespoons whole milk

1 pinch saffron strands

1 tablespoon rose water (*gulab jal*)

¼ cup chopped mixed nuts (pistachio and almonds), for garnish

To make the dates: Soak the dates in ½ cup of hot milk for 30 minutes. Set aside.

To make the rice: In a blender, pulse the rice with 2 tablespoons of milk until the rice is a grainy semolina-like consistency. The grains should feel coarse between your fingers.

In a large saucepan over medium heat, bring 3 cups of milk to a brisk boil. Add the rice and saffron while whisking continuously. Reduce the heat to low and keep stirring to thicken the mixture, about 20 minutes.

Simmer for another 20 to 25 minutes, until the mixture is thick and the rice cooked. Keep stirring to prevent sticking and lumps.

Stir in the dates and simmer for 3 to 4 minutes more. Finally, add the rose water and stir. Turn off the heat and let cool.

Spoon the pudding into small dessert glasses or bowls. Chill in the refrigerator for at least 3 hours, or overnight. Garnish with chopped pistachios or sliced almonds. Serve chilled.

Gajar Ka Halwa

SLOW-COOKED CARROT PUDDING WITH GHEE, MILK, AND CARDAMOM

YIELD: 6 TO 8 SERVINGS

A winter favorite, Gajar Ka Halwa is a rich and comforting Indian dessert made with grated carrots, milk, ghee, sugar, and nuts. Slow-cooked to perfection, this North Indian delicacy has a melt-in-your-mouth texture with a hint of cardamom. This dish takes me back to my childhood when my grandmother would serve warm *gajar halwa* with a drizzle of cream on cold winter nights!

½ cup whole almonds

4 tablespoons ghee

2 pounds carrots, peeled and grated

4 cups whole milk

¾ cup sugar

2 teaspoons cardamom powder

2 pinches saffron strands

Soak the almonds in hot water for 15 to 20 minutes. Peel, discard the skin, and thinly slice. Set aside.

Heat 2 tablespoons of ghee in a heavy-bottomed pan; add the carrots and sauté until they become slightly soft, 2 to 3 minutes.

Add the milk, turn the heat to medium-high, and bring the mixture to a boil. Turn the heat to low and cook until all the milk has evaporated, 45 minutes to 1 hour. Stir with a wooden spoon every time the milk froths up to keep the mixture from sticking.

At 20 minutes into this process, add the sugar and cook until the mixture has thickened.

When the mixture reaches a pudding-like consistency, at about 15 minutes, add the remaining 2 tablespoons of ghee, the cardamom powder, saffron strands, and sliced almonds. Simmer for 5 minutes more. Turn off the heat. Transfer to a serving bowl and serve hot or cold for a delicious dessert.

Sooji Halwa

QUICK, BUTTERY SEMOLINA PUDDING WITH SUGAR AND ALMONDS

YIELD: 6 TO 8 SERVINGS

A quick and comforting Indian sweet, Sooji Halwa is made with roasted, fine semolina (*sooji*), ghee, sugar, and nuts. It is often prepared during festivals, *poojas*, or simply as a quick dessert to satisfy a sweet craving. I love how it comes together in just 15 minutes, yet tastes so indulgent!

½ cup whole milk

¾ cup sugar

½ teaspoon saffron strands

½ cup ghee plus 1 tablespoon, for roasting

1 teaspoon cardamom powder

1 cup fine semolina (*sooji/rava*)

10 cashews, halved

2 tablespoons golden raisins

Add the milk, sugar, saffron, cardamom, and 2 cups of water to a saucepan over high heat. Bring to a boil and simmer, stirring regularly, until the sugar melts. Set aside.

In a wide, heavy-bottomed pan, heat ½ cup of ghee over medium heat; add the semolina (*rava/sooji*) and roast until the semolina turns a light golden-brown color, about 3 to minutes. Do not over-brown.

Gradually stir in the milk mixture. Take care to keep the heat at medium to minimize sputtering. Stir until the mixture thickens and pulls from the sides of the pan, about 10 minutes. Cover and simmer for 2 minutes more, stirring occasionally. Turn off the heat and let rest for 2 to 3 minutes.

In a separate small pan, heat 1 tablespoon of ghee over medium heat; add the cashews and golden raisins and roast until the cashew turn golden brown, about 1 minute.

Combine the cashews and golden raisins with the semolina mixture, stir well, and serve hot.

Traditional Shahi Tukda

ROYAL FRIED-BREAD PUDDING SOAKED IN SAFFRON MILK

YIELD: 6 TO 8 SERVINGS

A royal Mughlai dessert, Shahi Tukda is a rich and creamy bread pudding made with crispy fried bread slices soaked in rose-flavored sugar syrup and topped with thickened saffron milk. It's an ultimate indulgence, often served during Eid and at weddings. I love how this dessert is both simple and regal at the same time!

RABRI

4 cups whole milk

½ cup sugar

1 pinch of saffron strands

1 teaspoon cardamom powder

1 teaspoon rose water

SUGAR SYRUP

¼ cup sugar

½ teaspoon cardamom powder

1 tablespoon rose water

***SHAHI TUKDA* (FRIED BREAD)**

6 slices of bread, crusts removed and cut into diagonal slices

Ghee, for frying

2 tablespoons chopped almonds, for garnish

2 tablespoons chopped pistachios, for garnish

COOKING TIP

- Condensation will cause the cream from the milk to settle on the sides and bottom of the pan, which is why it's important to keep scraping down the cream and adding it back to the condensing milk. Stirring also prevents burning, which can ruin the taste of the *rabri*.

To make the rabri: In a saucepan over medium heat, add the milk, sugar, and saffron strands. Stir to combine and bring the mixture to a brisk boil. Boil for 2 to 3 minutes, turn the heat to low, and simmer, stirring continuously, until reduced by half. Scrape down the sides of the pan as the milk is condensing. Stir continuously to prevent burning and sticking. Turn off the heat. Add the cardamom powder and rose water and stir well. Set aside.

To make the sugar syrup: In a saucepan over medium heat, add the sugar and ¼ cup of water. Boil for 2 to 3 minutes, stirring until the sugar dissolves. Add the cardamom powder and rose water, stir, then turn off the heat.

To make the fried bread: Drizzle ghee generously over the bread pieces. Place them on a preheated pan and toast until golden and crisp on both sides. Set aside.

To serve, dip the fried bread slices in the sugar syrup, drain, and arrange on a serving dish. Pour the rabri over the top. Garnish with the chopped almonds and pistachios. Serve immediately.

Rice Kheer

CREAMY CARDAMOM-SCENTED RICE PUDDING SIMMERED IN FULL-FAT MILK

YIELD: 6 TO 8 SERVINGS

A classic Indian dessert, Rice Kheer, also known as Pal Payasam in the south, is a creamy and aromatic pudding made with slow-cooked rice, milk, sugar, and cardamom. It's a favorite during festivals, family gatherings, and celebrations. I remember enjoying a bowl of chilled kheer topped with slivered almonds as a child—it always felt like a treat!

1 tablespoon ghee

3 tablespoons basmati rice

4 cups whole milk

¼ cup sugar

NUTS

1 tablespoon ghee

10 cashews, halved

2 tablespoons golden raisins

Heat 1 tablespoon of ghee in a heavy-bottomed saucepan over medium heat. Add the rice and roast until you get a lightly roasted aroma, taking care not to brown the rice.

Add the milk and bring to a boil, then reduce the heat to low. Simmer the milk and rice mixture, stirring occasionally, until the milk reduces by half its quantity. Make sure the rice is cooked at this stage. Simmer longer, if needed. Lightly mash the rice while stirring with a spoon or spatula. Add the sugar and stir well until the sugar dissolves. Adjust the sugar according to taste. Transfer to a serving dish.

To make the nuts: Heat 1 tablespoon of ghee in a small pan over medium heat; add the cashews and golden raisins and roast until the cashews turn golden brown.

Stir into the kheer and serve warm or chilled.

Kesar Shrikhand

THICK, SILKY-SMOOTH SAFFRON YOGURT DESSERT WITH CARDAMOM

YIELD: 6 TO 8 SERVINGS

A classic Maharashtrian and Gujarati dessert, Kesar Shrikhand is a silky, thick, and sweetened yogurt delicacy flavored with saffron, cardamom, and nuts. It is light yet indulgent, often served as a festive dessert. I love how it pairs beautifully with *puris*, making it a traditional favorite for celebrations!

- 4 cups plain yogurt
- 1 cup sugar
- 1 large pinch of saffron strands
- ¼ teaspoon cardamom powder
- ¼ cup pistachios, shelled and finely chopped, for garnish

To make the *hung* yogurt: Line a strainer with a clean muslin cloth. Place the strainer over a deep bowl. Pour the yogurt into the bowl and bring the edges of the cloth up and tie them lightly to keep the curd from overflowing. Gently press and let the whey water drip out.

Keep the bowl set up in the refrigerator for about 15 hours, so most of the whey drips and collects in the bowl below. The result is a rich, creamy *hung* yogurt. Transfer to a large mixing bowl when ready.

Next, add the sugar, saffron, and cardamom powder into the jar of a blender and blend to a smooth powder.

Using a hand whisk, stir the sugar mixture into the yogurt and whisk until creamy and thick. Refrigerate for 2 hours for the flavors to infuse. The color will turn a lovely rich shade.

Scoop the yogurt into individual dessert bowls, top with crushed pistachios, and serve.

PAIRING SUGGESTIONS

Serve with Palak Paneer (page 95), Begun Bhaja (page 61), Gujarati Dal (page 79), Puri (page 135), Jeera Rice (page 118), and Palak Raita (page 157).

ACKNOWLEDGMENTS

Every journey in the kitchen begins with a single cutting board and a spark of curiosity. Mine started when I was just a child, standing on tiptoe beside my mother as she patiently guided my hands to whisk batter and chop vegetables. I vividly recall those early days—doing the so-called sous-chef tasks of washing greens, stirring pots, and measuring ingredients. At the tender age of twelve, I finally assembled my very first complete meal from start to finish, fueled by both nerves and excitement. That moment solidified my lifelong love for cooking and sharing meals with the people around me.

To my **dad**, who is no longer with us, your spirit of feeding and hosting people lives on in my heart. You showed me that cooking is an act of love—one that welcomes, warms, and nourishes. Thank you for instilling in me the same desire to live to eat and to feed others, ensuring every meal is a moment of connection.

To my **mom**, thank you for your gentle nurturing and for trusting a curious twelve-year-old with so many kitchen responsibilities. Your patience and unwavering belief in my ability have stayed with me, guiding every step of my culinary journey.

To my **brother**, who has never been shy about offering unfiltered feedback—every critique, whether gentle or blunt, pushed me to refine my skills and stay open to improvement. Your honesty helped me grow as both a cook and a creator.

To my **husband and our two boys**, thank you for being my enthusiastic taste-testers and biggest champions. You've sampled countless experimental dishes, endured my last-minute dinner ideas, and supported my passion through every success (and occasional kitchen flop). Your love and encouragement make each culinary adventure possible and more joyful.

To the **incredible fans of Archana's Kitchen**, you have brought so much joy and purpose to my cooking. Each time you try a new recipe, leave a thoughtful comment, or share your own adaptations, it reminds me why I started this journey in the first place. Your encouragement lights up my day and propels me to dream bigger, cook better, and share more.

Finally, to everyone who believes that a home-cooked meal can be a source of warmth, connection, and love: This book is for you. May it inspire you to create cherished memories in your own kitchen, just as I did many years ago, perched at the counter next to my mom—learning, experimenting, and discovering the magic of Indian cooking.

INDEX

S

T

V

Y

Z

ABOUT THE AUTHOR

Archana Doshi is the founder of *Archana's Kitchen*, India's leading food and recipe platform, which reaches millions of home cooks every month. A self-taught cook and passionate food educator, Archana began her culinary journey in her mother's kitchen—chopping, whisking, and cleaning long before she learned to make a complete meal at the age of twelve.

Over the years, her love for everyday home cooking evolved into a mission: to make Indian food simple, wholesome, and accessible to everyone. Through her website, books, and videos, she has inspired home cooks across the world to rediscover the joy of cooking with fresh ingredients, balanced flavors, and a touch of tradition.

Archana lives in Bangalore with her husband and two sons, who are her biggest food critics and supporters. Her late father's love for feeding people and her mother's love for hosting guests remains her deepest inspiration—reminding her every day that food is more than a meal; it's how we share love.

When she's not testing recipes or teaching others to cook, Archana can be found planning her next meal, exploring local markets, or sharing stories of Indian food culture with her global audience.

weldon**owen**

an imprint of Insight Editions
P.O. Box 3088
San Rafael, CA 94912
www.weldonowen.com

CEO Raoul Goff
VP Publisher Roger Shaw
Executive Editor Edward Ash-Milby
Assistant Editor Kayla Belser
Managing Editor Michelle Hope
Art Director & Designer Megan Sinead Bingham
Production Design Jean Hwang
VP Manufacturing Alix Nicholaeff
Senior Production Manager Joshua Smith
Strategic Production Planner Lina s Palma-Temena

Photographer Stacy Ventura
Food Stylist Victoria Woollard
Food Stylist Assistant Allee Cakmis
Prop Styling Megan Sinead Bingham

Weldon Owen would also like to thank Margaret Parrish and Crystal Coppock.

ISBN: 979-8-88674-286-2

Manufactured in China by Weldon Owen
10 9 8 7 6 5 4 3 2 1

Insight Editions, in association with Roots of Peace, will plant two trees for each tree used in the manufacturing of this book. Roots of Peace is an internationally renowned humanitarian organization dedicated to eradicating land mines worldwide and converting war-torn lands into productive farms and wildlife habitats. Roots of Peace will plant two million fruit and nut trees in Afghanistan and provide farmers there with the skills and support necessary for sustainable land use.